D1490987

APHRODISIACS
AND
LOVE MAGIC

APHRODISIACS AND LOVE MAGIC

PAMELA ALLARDICE

PRISM · UNITY

Thanks, Mum

Published in Great Britain 1989 by:
PRISM PRESS
2 South Street,
Bridport,
Dorset DT6 3NQ

and distributed in the USA by:
AVERY PUBLISHING GROUP INC.,
350 Thorens Avenue,
Garden City Park,
New York 11040

and published in Australia 1989 by:
UNITY PRESS,
6a Ortona Road
Lindfield,
NSW 2070

ISBN 1 85327 031 8

© 1989 Pamela Allardice

Printed and bound in the Channel Islands
by The Guernsey Press Limited.

TABLE OF CONTENTS

INTRODUCTION

More than any other aspects of our lives, love and marriage are governed by a wealth of superstitions, rituals and magic.

Lovers seek lucky omens and observe ancient customs, and the wedding ceremony itself has many old traditions which are still kept up, even when those taking part are unaware of their significance.

Love charms and spells were traditionally the domain of young women in years gone by, whose concern was motivated by the seclusion in which they were forced to live. In many cases, a young girl had little or no choice in the selection of her future husband, even though marriage was the only accept-able future for her.

The fear of being 'left on the shelf' hung over rich and poor alike in all different cultures — spinsters assiduously searched for hopeful omens, petitioned the appropriate gods and brewed fantastic and noisome potions to avoid this fate.

A LITTLE LOVE LORE

Lust-provoking philtres were concocted by the ancients of Assyria, Persia and China, with the earliest recorded recipes coming from undated Egyptian medical papyri from the Middle Kingdom, between 2200–1700 B.C. The greatest adepts were the Greek women of Thessaly, which was the home of magic and the cult of the arch-sorceress Medea. Seneca, the Roman dramatist, portrays her brewing up:

"... venom extracted from serpents, entrails and organs of unclean birds, the heart of a screech owl and vampire's vitals, ripped from living flesh."

... in her cauldron by moonlight.

An infamous ingredient was hippomanes, a small piece of flesh taken from the forehead of a newly foaled colt. Caesonia, wife of Caligula, gave the demented Roman emperor a potion of powdered hippomanes, mixed with his own blood, which made:

"... the blood run hissing through his veins, till the mad vapour mounted to his brains."

English country folk still say that a drop of blood from a man's little finger put in a woman's wine will make her fall passionately in love with him. This belief has its origins in fetishism, or sympathetic magic, which specified nail parings, bones and pieces of clothing as ingredients in love charms. For instance:

"Take three pubic hairs and three from the left armpit. Burn them on a hot shovel, pulverise and insert them in a piece of

bread to be fed to the lover."
Albertus Magnus, medieval occultist

Cow dung was used by the American Apache Indians, and even human excrement, long regarded as excellent protection against ghosts and evil spirits in many cultures, has been associated with love magic. Another favourite ingredient has been human or animal semen — not surprisingly, given its high hormone content.

Sympathetic magic has resulted in man's conscious and sub-conscious beliefs that by eating the flesh of certain animals, he will assume their valued characteristics. For instance, a lion's heart will bestow bravery, venison will encourage fleetness of foot, and eating that traditional fertility symbol, the rabbit, will result in many children. The latter logic led to the custom of carrying or touching a rabbit's foot for luck — for the foot, a phallic symbol, coupled with the prolific rabbit, was a token of creativity and positive outcomes.

Reindeer have been hotly pursued by Chinese and Russians until quite recently. Both cultures swear by a brew of alcoholic brine and powdered reindeer antlers, said to have been imbibed by Czars and Emperors alike for its extraordinary effect upon male performance. Maoris make a tonic from the velvet skin scraped from the deer's antlers, hoping this will help them emulate the animal's famed, unflagging sexual appetite.

Civet deer were also prized trophies in many cultures, for their glands yielded the pungent fragrance of musk. This earthy, sexy smell enjoyed a resurgence of popularity during the hippie heyday of Haight-Ashbury in 1960s America.

Elephants were hunted unmercifully for their tusks, as powdered ivory was mistakenly held to be a potent restorative. Ditto the poor rhino — although ground rhino horn is no longer legally sold, its legacy, the word "horny", indicates the esteem it was held in.

The ancient Hindus, renowned for their book on love "The

Kama Sutra", recommended the flesh of a baby white heifer to be cooked in its mother's milk for an aphrodisiac effect. The English have always admired the fox for its courage and sheer cheekiness, so a young lad who was less than successful with the local lasses would wear a dried fox's tongue around his neck as an amulet to encourage him to be bold and dashing. The most famous animal in traditional love lore is, however, the skink. The Persians hunted it to prepare a love potion by mixing its flesh with amber, ground pearls, saffron and opium. It is still used in Eastern medicine, primarily as an antidote to poison.

The sexual organs of animals, particularly horses, bulls and sheep, were believed to stimulate the sexual drive. Scottish seers sometimes used the blade-bones and testicles of a black sheep in love divination. All the flesh had first to be scraped off the bone without the aid of iron, for if an iron or steel object touched it, its magic was lost. The magician would then ask his subject to hold the bone over his shoulder in the direction of the Highland's greatest length. The sheep's testicles would be burned and a hazel wand dipped in the ashes before being rubbed over the broad end of the bone, thus highlighting marks on the bone which would answer the enquirer's questions.

Throughout the world, bizarre ingredients have been manufactured from long-suffering animals — aesthetically pleasing, though fiddly to prepare was the Chinese method whereby butterflies' wings were crushed with honey, pressed into small balls and slipped into the loved one's clothing or food. A Louisiana Creole recipe also employs butterflies' wings, this time grinding them to a powder with a toasted hummingbird heart "for amorous results".

More often, though, quite horrible charms were employed where small animal-victims were tortured in order to bring corresponding pain in some human being. Thought to promote love and to have magical healing properties, young frogs feature in many aphrodisiac recipes — possibly because they were easily captured by young girls who had to negotiate voluminous skirts and corsets. To cure a love-sick girl, a live frog was pinned in a box until it died and withered. The little, key-shaped bone was then removed from its chest and hooked onto the coat of the desired lover, while these words were recited:

> "I do not wish to hurt thee, frog
> But my true lover's heart to turn;
> Wishing that he no rest may find,
> Until he comes and speaks his mind."

A girl whose lover was untrue could stick pins all over a living frog and bury it. The young man would then suffer extreme pain in all his limbs and would have to return to her for only by marrying her would the pain abate.

Another singularly unpleasant Lincolnshire charm involved an unlucky toad. The girl had to go to Communion service and keep the bread in her mouth until the service was over. When she came out of church, she would find a toad waiting for her. She then had to give the moist bread to the toad to eat and the next time she met her unwitting sweetheart, he would be helpless to her charms and ask her to marry him. The same rite could also be used by those desirous of becoming witches.

A pigeon's heart could be stuck with iron nails and secreted up a chimney to recall a straying lover. To ensure he stayed put, he would then be fed a soup containing sesame oil and vinegar in which a crow's feather had been dipped. If, a little dazed from the effects of so much magic, the fellow was unable to perform to the girl's satisfaction, the following ointment from a medieval 'grimoire', or spell-book, had spectacular results:

> "Add of three-yeris old goat ye left testycle and from ye back heyres of a whyte whelp. Infuse alle ye items in a bottel halfe fylled with brandye. Cook on ye twenty-firste daye, add three droppes of crocodile semen and passe through fylter till thicke consystence is reched."

6

Logically progressing from charms and potions designed to capture a partner, many nostrums doubled up as fertility-inducing agents for childless couples. A typical example was "The Mixture to Promote Breeding", published in "The Compleat Housewife" in London, in 1753. This was based on three pints of strong ale, in which was boiled three ox-testicles, 'ox-backs' (the animal's spinal marrow), catmint, sliced dates, stoned raisins, three whole nutmegs 'prick'd full of holes' and 'the syrup of stinking orris'.

In some parts of the world, a woman who has failed to conceive within a reasonable time after marriage is beaten with a stick, which has been previously used to separate mating dogs. By this means, the fertility and lustful intent of the animals is transferred to the human. However, lest it be thought that the woman always comes off second-best, the fault is often ascribed to the man, particularly if he has a small penis. In Brazil, a man will be ordered to belabour himself with twigs from the Gninga tree, a prolific river plant, in the hope that he may 'branch out' as strongly as it does. An African tribal fertility rite could well instil panic in a Western male. There, the tip of the penis would have been slit and packed with fine pebbles and sand; as it healed over, it was believed to give additional pleasure to the wife, and to encourage conception. A tamer version comes from the supposedly staid Victorians, who would pop a feather into the end of the penis, though in China both parties would have been dourly advised to abstain from sex for a spell, or dosed with some caustic laxative treatment, for good measure.

More obscure is the theory that contact with a dead human body, particularly that of a criminal, will induce fertility. In 17th century England, the hands and feet of a gallows corpse were much in demand from childless couples as a love charm to place under their bed, while in the American Deep South, there is still a lingering belief in what was originally an old British superstition, that white moss taken from the skull of a murdered man has special magical properties as an aphro-disiac. In Ireland, too, a besotted lad might have been driven to grave-digging — having stolen a hair from the head of his beloved, he would then thread it on a needle, dig up some poor corpse and pass the needle through its arm. This would make him irresistible to his girl, both in this life and the next.

Other ghoulish beliefs centre on that element staple to life — water. Water has always been associated with fertility rites in all cultures, be they Christian or pagan. As head-hunters, the Celts revered the severed head as a powerful trophy and talisman, and would throw them into wells, springs and pools in the belief that the water therein would then have the power of promoting life. For instance, St. Winifred's Well in England is named for a beautiful virgin who was summarily decapitated by her rejected suitor. Her head rolled down a hill and, where it came to rest, a spring burst forth, which for centuries has been visited by both barren men and lonely women.

PLANTING AN AMOROUS GARDEN

True romantics should take heed of the lore surrounding various trees and plants before sowing their garden. No matter how large or small the plot available, a girl can take the upper hand in affairs of the heart through a little judicious planting. Herbs, in particular, have long been recommended as fertility agents — which is scarcely surprising, given their accessibility and man's ever-present primeval instinct to propagate the race. They have a very ancient reputation for restoring youth and vigour, and there are constant references in early literature, especially from Greek and Roman times, to rejuvenating herbal baths for older men containing alfalfa, peppermint and angelica. While some may argue that the effect is purely psychological, I have it on the best authority that a warming herbal tisane or liqueur at bedtime is just the thing to restore the drive and stimulate the nervous system.

Herbs

Seventeenth century herbalists set great store by those herbal 'simples' which helped to drive away 'melancholy'. This flight into the world of ideal love and harmony was very likely a reaction to the widespread depression and anxiety of the times, for it was an age seething with political unrest and intrigue, so tonics were often prescribed 'to comfort the heart'.

For example, flowers of the salad burnet were recommended by Gerard 'to make the heart merrie and glad'. Borage was another of his favourite herbs; he relied upon it 'to drive away sorrow by force and vertue'. The ancient Greeks concurred: they named borage 'Euphrosynon', alleging that quaffing the juice fermented in wine made the drinker happy, as well as providing sexual stimulation. John Evelyn, who was as much interested in simples as in 'sallets', recommended sprigs of borage to 'revive the heartsicke' and the brilliant blue starry blooms were embroidered on scarves by womenfolk and presented to their knights before battle. During the age of chivalry, borage tea was given to knights before a jousting tournament to give them strength.

Besides the traditional favourites which follow, malefern, periwinkle, wild poppy, juniper, elecampane and endive are all considered to be of an erotic nature. Mrs. Leyel says that these were often combined with herbs that were poisonous if taken in too great quantities — presumably, one then died of a broken heart.

Parkinson referred to Southernwood as 'maiden's ruin', but the reference made to it by herbalist William Coles was far more condemnatory:

> "It is said that if a bunch of southernwood be laid under one's pillow, bed or bolster, it provoketh carnall copulation and resisteth all enchantments that hinder same."

It was thought that if a girl put a sprig of southernwood down her back before leaving the house in the morning, she would marry the first boy she met; or, if she put it under her pillow, she would dream of the man she was to wed.

St. John's Wort, which looks like a little sun and blooms around Midsummer's Day in the northern hemisphere, was a magical plant in almost every country where it was known. This poem is translated from the German ballad:

> "The young maid stole from the cottage door
> And blushed as she sought the plant of power
> 'Thou silver glow-worm, lend me thy light
> I must gather the mystic St. John this night
> The wonderful herb whose leaf shall decide
> If the coming year shall make me a bride."

She had to then sleep with the flowers and leaves under her mattress and she would dream of the man she would marry, and when. Similarly, if a childless wife walked naked around her garden at midnight to pick the flowers, she would have a child before the next St. John's Eve came around.

Yarrow, or milfoil, is a witches' herb and used in many divination spells. Even today in France and Ireland, it is thought that yarrow leaves held over the eyes give second sight, and it may be used by the lovelorn and lonely to conjure a vision of a future sweetheart. Sometimes called Bloodwort, as it was used to staunch a bleeding nose, it could actually be used to cause bleeding by thrusting a leaf up the nostril and wiggling it about. English girls did this as a form of divination, saying:

"Yarroway, yarroway, bear a white blow
If my love loves me, my nose will bleed now.
If my love don't love me, it won't bleed a drop,
If my love do love me, 'twill bleed every drop."

A Welsh girl would sew yarrow in a red flannel pouch and place it under her pillow to dream of her future mate. However, this spell would only be successful if she had gathered the yarrow from a young man's grave, murmuring as she did so:

"Yarrow, sweet yarrow, the first I have found,
In the name of Jesus Christ, I pluck it from the ground.
As Jesus lov'd sweet Mary and took her for his dear,
So, in a dream this night, may my true love appear."

Though young women were not permitted to walk in hemp-fields in case they became barren, they could put the seed to good use in marriage divination. To see the apparition of her future husband, a girl had to visit the church at midnight and walk backwards to her home from the porch, scattering hemp-seed as she recited:

"Hempseed I sow, hempseed I throw
Let my true love come after me and mow."

If nothing happened, it meant she would not marry that year, or perhaps not at all. If she was destined to die young and unwed, a spectral coffin would be seen following her instead of the hoped-for-man.

The four-leafed clover is, traditionally, the luckiest, and it is said that if a young man or woman finds one, they can expect to meet their true love that day. Its reputation springs from the legend that Eve took one with her when she was expelled from paradise, with God blessing it as follows:

"One leaf for fame, one leaf for wealth
One leaf for a faithful lover,
And one leaf to bring most glorious health —
All in God's four-leafed clover."

Incidentally, a four-leafed clover is only lucky if it is found by accident; consciously seeking one will destroy its power. Don't despair if you only find a three-leafed one, for in Ireland this is actually the most powerful version, having been selected by St. Patrick to illustrate the doctrine of the Holy Trinity. A two leafed clover also has its place in love lore and divination:

"A clover, a clover of two
Put it in your right shoe.
The first young man you meet,
In field, lane or street
You'll have him, or one of his name."

In the 19th century, Gloucestershire girls used turf in a rather morbid form of divination. A green bough, a bowl of water and a piece of turf were laid out and each girl, blindfolded, had to crawl towards them on hands and knees. To touch the turf first meant the poor lass would die before she was married, while the bough was not much better — to touch this first meant she would be a widow.

Mandrake is mentioned in the Song of Solomon as a cure for sterility, and Leah even used it to seduce Jacob in the Book of Genesis, while the ancient Egyptian word for this peculiar plant translates as "phallus of the field". A popular ingredient in many witches' brews and love potions in the Middle Ages, its long, forked root was said to embody a demon. Dogs were tied to the plant and used to uproot it, for any man who heard the demon shriek as it was wrenched from the ground would die in agony.

In the Northern English counties, the male and female briony are still often called "mandrake" and "womandrake" respectively. The plant was thought to have strong aphrodisiac properties and witches used it in their spells to induce fertility in both people and horses, chanting as they dosed their subject:

> "If to childe-bede thou wouldst goe,
> dust thy food with brionie."

Garlic, in addition to being a time-honoured anti-biotic, is also considered one of the most versatile herbal aphrodisiacs of all. The strong-smelling antiseptic oil will tone up the body organs, cleanse the blood and bestow strength — qualities which every Mediterranean Romeo well knows.

Springwort was the name given to caper spurge, a magical plant associated with fire and power. If buried on a mountain top, it was said to 'bring down the lightning and divide the storm'. For this reason, medieval Frenchmen would rub it on their limbs to gain superhuman sexual strength while women ate it to ensure fecundity.

The name vervain means, in Latin, 'sacred herb', while its classical definition 'herba veneris', refers to its lust-provoking powers. Used extensively by priests to decorate altars in temples and in homes, witches and magicians also called upon it to assist with seduction plans. Virgil wrote in Book VIII of Eclogues:

"Burn rich vervain and frankincense
that I may array with magic spell
to turn my cold lover's mood to passion."

In his charming "Ode to Phyllis", Horace beseeches his mistress to live with him, offering:

". . . my house shining with silver,
the halls twined with wreaths of holy vervain."

However, vervain was not always considered a lucky herb, nor especially favourable for women. A 16th century writer says bitterly of his erstwhile ladylove:

"Thou art like the veruen
— poyson one way and pleasure an other."

It has returned to favour in more recent times; today a traditionally-minded young German bride will wake on her wedding day to a cup of vervain tea, and a piece will often be slipped into her bodice or waistband for luck.

Valerian was once considered a powerful aphrodisiac. In one account, the Pied Piper of Hamelin lured rats with a pocketful of valerian, for it was said to attract animals as well as arousing lust in humans. In the Middle Ages, its rather animal scent was considered pleasing — perfumes were made from the flowers and the leaves used to sweeten linen. A memory of its use as a love charm still exists in Wales, where it is said that if a girl slips a sprig of valerian into her camisole when dressing, she will never lack for suitors.

Comfrey, which is universally respected for its ability to heal broken bones and skin, was a most important inclusion to the herb garden of a medieval maid ruing the loss of her virginity. Contemporary practitioners assured her that sitting for an hour in a warm decoction of this plant's leaves would 'repair the irretrievable damage of love.'

Speaking of 'rue', this herb, though better known for its associations with death and heartbreak, does have a surprising though contradictory effect on the sexes, according to Sir John Harington:

"This noble hearbe (while) making men chaste,
women fils with luste."

Ancient physicians deemed Lady's Mantle to have super-natural restorative powers for womens' problems. Its country name resulted from the belief that it had the blessing of Our Lady, and it was taken to help conception and protect the unborn child, a reputation enhanced by Culpeper who said:

"Lady's Mantle inspyres lust to the work of generacyon . . ."

He also commented obscurely about another female tonic herb, tansy:

"Let those women who desire children love this herb. It is their best companion, their husbands excepted."

and recommended that it be fried with eggs "to digest and carry downward those bad humours that trouble the stomach."

It is said that after a battle or plague, Hippocrates would prescribe the use of sage tea for all Greek womenfolk, to make them more fertile and thus replenish the country's losses. English superstition has twisted this somewhat, saying that sage bestows unnatural strength of will upon women — therefore, a credulous man would be likely to cut down a too-healthy sage bush, for fear his neighbours might think he was not the master in his own house.

Similarly, parsley has an unexpected dark domestic side. An ingredient in witches' flying ointments and believed "to grow rank in a cuckold's garden", even today it is believed that if a man is unable to grow this simple herb his wife will wear the pants. A mass of other superstitions to do with festivity and fertility were associated with parsley. The ancient Greeks loved it well, and a Theocritan lover would wear a parsley wreath at a

15

banquet, believing the green tendrils made him more attractive, as well as warding off inebriation. It was considered particularly lucky if parsley was found growing naturally near a house, as it ensured many healthy children would be born there for as long as the plant lived. In fact, according to popular folklore, a woman who is given a parsley plant will bear a child within twelve months and English children are sometimes told that the doctor digs new babies up from the parsley bed, rather than the gooseberry bush. However, other folklore contradicts these positive attributes, saying that unmarried girls who inadvertently become pregnant should eat parsley three days running in the hope of escaping from their predicament.

Fennel was a favourite love herb at one time, albeit with a sad history. Said to be beloved by Adonis, its relatively short life signified the brief affair between this god and the goddess of love, Aphrodite. It was woven into garlands and chaplets worn by Greek youths at the annual fete to Adonis, and Parkinson recommended it be:

". . . boyled in Barley water and drunk for Nurses to encrease their milke."

Used by the ladies of the harems in North Africa and the Middle East as a stimulant to conception, fenugreek has the happy side effect of "encouraging alluring roundness of the breast." Czech peasant girls wore small bags of lovage and fenugreek seeds around their necks when they were with their sweethearts, since they considered both to be potent love charms. They may well have not been mistaken in their beliefs, for modern-day research has proved lovage, at least, to be a good natural deodorant, which may account for its traditional success.

The Latin name for savory — satureia — came from the legend that the lascivious satyrs of mythology soaked the leaves in their cups of wine. Herbalists have long referred to its lust-provoking power; in particular, they have recommended

16

savory boiled in wine for womens' disorders, because of its favourable effect on the reproductive system.

Pennyroyal flowers were given as a tea to aid many female complaints and the Greek historian Ovid claimed feverfew to have a specific aphrodisiac effect on women. Although modern herbalists do not go this far, they do laud the plant for its positive and stimulating effect on the nervous system and it has been proved to have the ability to control migraines. Another aphrodisiac from Classical times was rocket, an offering always sown around the shrine of the phallic god, Priapus.

Many herbal gynaecological treatments double up as female aphrodisiacs, presumably because of their relaxing effect on the reproductive system. Burdock was chosen by Venus for her own, according to Culpeper, due to its ability "to pull the wombe which way you please". Similarly, the Greco–Roman use of mugwort tea as a tonic for young girls held true in medieval times, as evidenced by the proverb:

"If they would drink nettles in March and eat mugwort in May
so many fine maids would na go to the clay."

One of the old herbalists, Drayton, was even more specific, claiming:

"The belly hurt by birth, by mugwort to make sound."

Red raspberry leaf tea was used for the same purpose. Taken warm and combined with cinnamon bark, it is still prescribed by midwives today to facilitate childbirth. On the other side of the world, the pretty and fragrant white flowers of the squaw bush were favoured by Red Indian maidens of the Iroquoi and Cree tribes to aid conception and help produce an easy labour.

Spices

Spices were feared by the English Puritans because of their ability to "provoke unseemly passion". Considering the eventual overthrow of their regime, they could well have had cause to fear these substances. Oriental cultures, however, had few such qualms, and many favourite spices hail from the mystical East.

The delights of saffron have been extolled since Biblical times, being heralded in the Song of Solomon:

> "A garden is my bride . . .
> Thy shoots are an orchard of pomegranates
> with precious fruits.
> Henna with spikenard plants,
> spikenard and saffron . . ."

The ancient Phoenicians ate crescent-shaped cakes flavoured with this spice at festivals to honour their goddess of love, fertility and harvest, Ashtoreth. Vicinius in "Quo Vadis" says that when he builds a house for his beloved, he will erect an altar, as to a divinity, offering myrrh and aloes and, in the springtime, apple blossom and saffron. Long used as a symbol of station and luxury because of its cost, he also refers to a marriage banquet where the guests were showered with the golden powder from nets suspended from the ceiling.

Medieval herbalists were more definite about the amorous powers of saffron. "The virtue thereof", said Christopher Catton "pierceth the heart, provoking laughter and merriment", while Lord Bacon added "it maketh the English sprightly" (. . . no small feat, one would suggest). The botanist Ray echoed their sentiments, writing:

> ". . . it has long enjoyed the reputation of comforting the heart
> and raising the spirits, going far towards the relief of those who
> are melancholy or heartsicke."

Interestingly, modern scientific experiments in both China

and America now indicate that saffron does indeed stimulate the uterus and quicken the heartbeat.

A traditional Chinese love spice, nutmeg has a great strengthening effect, when brewed into a hot tea. Caraway has been a popular ingredient in love potions since it was prescribed by the great Greek physician Dioscorides for young girls who were "pale and wan". Perhaps its greatest merit is its ability to ease digestion at bedtime — an asset utilised by the lusty Sir John Falstaff in his seduction plans:

> "You shall see my orchard where, in an arbour we will eat a last pippin of my own grafting with a dish of caraways . . . and then to bed!"

The herb basil was often associated with love potions. In parts of Northern Europe, it was used to test whether a girl was still a virgin — she had to walk through a swarm of bees holding basil in her hands. If the bees attacked her, or the plant withered in her hands, she was unchaste on two counts. Shelley wrote:

> "Madonna, wherefore hast thou sent me
> Sweet basil and mignonette?
> Embleming love and health which never yet
> In the same wreath might be?"

Sacred to Erzulie, the Haitian goddess of voodoo love magic, basil was often cited as an aid to childbirth. In Italy, basil meant "love' and its country name translated literally as "Kiss Me, Nicholas". Its reputation is, however, inconsistent — some herbalists have spoken well of it, others swear it is unfit for men to eat. Witness Culpeper's abstruse comment:

> ". . . as it helps the deficiency of Venus in one kind,
> So it spoils all her actions in another. I dare write no more of it."

Dill features in many cook books and vegetable gardens, old and new, as a popular flavouring agent for soups, salads and pickles. In medieval times, it was considered a protective against the spells of witches and gypsies and, when steeped in wine, a potent aphrodisiac and love philtre. An infusion of the seeds is also a time-honoured remedy for colic in children. A similar infusion, which has had a broth of celery seeds stirred through it three times, was specifically recommended for men who could not perform, and gypsy women recommended a poultice of the leaves to make the breasts of nursing mothers full and round.

Today, Chinese midwives will still offer a new mother a piece of ginger, which has been soaked in hot wine, immediately after she has given birth to a son. Perhaps this tradition may trace its origins to the ancient Greeks — they offered the heart-warmingly spicy pickled root to couples who had been unable to have a child.

Thyme was another aphrodisiac of Grecian birth. It was said to have been worn in young girls' wreaths as they gathered honey from the hives on Mount Hymettus. Up-to-the-minute herbalists still use it as a sedative — its calming, soothing effect could well reduce nervousness in a potential suitor.

Coriander was first mentioned as an aphrodisiac in "The Arabian Nights". It also achieved notoriety during medieval times when lads took advantage of their lasses after having dosed them with copious quantities of this spice — for, when consumed in excess, coriander has a slightly narcotic effect, hence its country name, "Dizzy Corn".

"Hot" spices are traditionally popular aphrodisiacs, adding fire to seductive recipes and to the heart. Chilis and chili powder should be treated with caution, as should mustard and pepper in excess. They owe their reputation to their irritating effect on the urinary tract. As with Spanish fly, a quite dangerous and illegal powder made from the ground Cantharides beetle, such substances can give a man an erection, whether his thoughts are on sex, or not. Such hot spices were given to unwilling animals in the past, for they would mate simply to get rid of the discomfort.

Flowers

As with 'gynaecological' herbs and spices, many heavily scented or brightly-coloured flowers are traditionally potent aphrodisiacs — no doubt as a result of their ability to create a voluptuous, seductive mood.

Purple cyclamen flowers were incorporated in little cakes which, when eaten, Gerard tells us, "made a goodly amorous medicine'. In the 1930s, Dr Edward Bach used fuschia essence in his flower remedies to treat sexual inertia and as an aid to a girl recovering from the shock of being jilted. The ancient Greeks used the roots and flowers of the morning glory vine in an aphrodisiac tonic called scammony, and chewed the seeds for their supposed extraordinary orgasmic sensation — to their chagrin, we must suppose, for these are harsh purgatives.

Tobacco plant and night-scented stock are reputed to be sexual stimulants, as is the creamy yellow Eastern "Queen of the Flowers", ylang-ylang, which Indian doctors prescribe to overcome impotence, and frigidity. Chinese women believed the exquisite fragrance of jasmine attracted men, and threaded the florets through their hair, while Gauguin referred to Tahitian girls using the tiare flower for the same purpose — from whence came our word, 'tiara'.

Attar of roses, rose oil, rose vinegar and rose water were all ingredients in medieval love philtres. A popular Roman tonic for a love-sick maiden or youth was dried rose and violet petals, saffron, myrrh, lavender and rosemary, mixed with the flesh of a viper and stirred with honey, while the following delightful love charm comes from Germany:

> "Take three roses — white, pink and red. Wear them next to your heart for three days. Steep them in wine for three days more, then give to your lover. When he drinks, he will be yours forever."

Poppy and rose petals may be used to determine if a lover is faithful to you in two ways. If a curved petal of either flower splits when you stick it to your forehead, the person you have 'in mind' loves you truly. Similarly, if a petal placed in the palm of your hand splits with a popping noise when you hit it with the other fist, he is in love with you.

Trees

I think I must have been a dryad in a previous life, for I love trees so, experiencing a real pang when one has to be pruned. Here are a few favourites, which augur well for an amorous garden:

The apple has symbolised fruitfulness and been employed to divine the future since the days of medieval England. Lancelot was sleeping under a magic apple tree when the four fairy queens spirited him away and Arthur's last resting place was said to have been Avalon, or the Isle of Apples.

Games abound whereby a girl may select her future husband from a number of options, or divine who he might be. For instance, apple pips can help her choose if she is beset by several lovers. For each suitor, she should take a pip and drop it on the fire. If it goes off with a popping sound, then its namesake is 'bursting' with love for her; if it makes no noise, then he is not truly in love. She could also try pressing an apple pip to her cheek as she recites a list of possible mates, for the name she says as the pip drops off will be that of her future husband.

Another game involves peeling the skin off an apple in one long piece and tossing this over the left shoulder. If the peel stays in one unbroken strip, it should fall in the shape of a letter, and this will be the initial of the future partner. If it breaks, there will be no marriage at all.

Along with the apple, many other trees, being the home of elves and fairies, have supernatural powers which may be enlisted by humans. The oak, in particular, has been regarded as a sacred tree from earliest times, and the magical acorn can be used to test love. Two should be floated in a bowl of water and, if they bob together, then the couple who placed them will marry; if they do not, the people concerned will drift apart.

The ash tree has an important place in any garden, and has been associated with many love games and divination spells. Its magical reputation stems from ancient writings of the Norse holy men. They believed that the first man on earth was named Askr, because he was created from an ash tree.

One of the most popular games involves the ash's winged seeds — they have to be gathered by moonlight, as the following verse is recited:

> "Even ash, even ash, I pluck thee
> This night my true love to see,
> Neither in his bed nor in the bare,
> But in the clothes he does everyday wear."

The third seed picked should be placed in the enquirer's left shoe and worn thus, hidden under the foot. The first young man met thereafter will be the future husband.

An English divination game for winter-time entails binding green ash twigs together and placing them on the fire to burn. Each twig is named for an unmarried girl in the household, and she whose band breaks first will be the first to wed.

Pear trees were used by girls keen to catch a glimpse of the man of their dreams. On Christmas Eve, a girl had to walk backwards to the tree, then around it three times while holding a willow wand straight out in front of her. As she recited:

> "He that's to be my gude man, come and grip the end on't"

the wraith of her future husband would be seen, holding the end of the stick.

Tropical Plants

Native to hot countries, there are many tropical plants and trees — cotton root, palm, hygrophila, matica and muira-pama, for example — that are all prescribed for their aphrodisiac properties. If you live in a tropical area, or even just have a particularly sunny nook in your garden, you might like to experiment with some of the more exotic plants.

The bamboo plant has been used as an aphrodisiac in Asia, where native witch doctors use the shoots in a potion to produce clairvoyance and a state of ecstasy. An important part of Malay natives' diet is the durian fruit, which is also valued as a powerful aphrodisiac, as evidenced by this piece of local doggerel:

> ". . . when the durian falls,
> the sarong rises."

Though many people do enjoy the taste, likening it to rich, almond-flavoured custard, it does have a penetrating and most offensive odour which needs to be overcome before it can be used for its amatory properties.

Another Malay aphrodisiac is sago broth or gruel, particularly prescribed as a restorative for an aging chief; while in India, rumi-mastaki, or mastic, is combined with jalap for the same purpose. The best mastic traditionally came from the island of Scio, where the Turkish masters limited its cultivation to chosen subjects, awarding the use of the gum to worthy people only. In Malaya, it is combined with opium, sago, honey and aromatic herbs as a beverage to be served at wedding feasts — interestingly, this is yet another quite drastic purgative, which irritates the genitals, possibly accounting for its success.

Kava-kava root is used to prepare a national aphrodisiac beverage by the Fijian and Samoan natives. The drink produces a pleasant form of intoxication, followed by a tranquil condition and incoherent, uninhibited dreams.

Saw palmetto grows best along the South Eastern coast of the United States of America. The berry, acting as a tonic to the reproductive tissues and mucous membranes, was widely used as a love food by the Negro slaves until the late 18th century. The plant's reputation lingers on, however, as farmers continue to add it to their stock feed to make their cows fat, sleek and fertile.

Marijuana is probably one of the most controversial aphrodisiacs of recent times. A native of India and other hot places, it has long been used as a relaxant in many cultures, for the resin of the flower bracts is intoxicating and hallucinatory. Its Indian name is 'charas', meaning 'the laughter mover' or 'exciter of desire', a reference to its use in amatory rites.

"The legal alternative to marijuana", ginseng is another exotic plant with aphrodisiac properties. Its root resembles a mandrake plant in appearance, and the ancient Chinese improved upon this image by carving male and female genitalia in the appropriate spot. Its main claims are to slow the aging process and give stamina and endurance. The Chinese say that, in order for ginseng to be effective, it must be dug up at midnight under a full moon. They believe it to be a powerful restorative and tonic, claiming it prolongs life and benefits the lungs, heart, spleen and kidneys.

In Mexico, damiana, a small, mint-like plant with yellowish fragrant flowers, is much used as an aphrodisiac, either alone or prescribed with other herbs. This plant contains high levels of phosphorus, which would account for its ability to overcome lassitude and loss of nervous energy. Native Mexicans from the arid Coahuila province will give a potion containing gobernadora leaves to a young boy to drink as part of his initiation to manhood. It is claimed to make him as strong and powerful as the mountain ram who eats it.

Sweet-scented musk seeds were traditionally prepared into a tincture, combined with jasmine oil and used to anoint Hindu brides on their wedding night. Both the milk and dried kernels of coconuts have been used in Hindu love potions, while the toddy obtained from date palms is given to young women trying to conceive as a substitute for coffee. Both the coconut and date palms, bearing many fruit in any one season and often continuing to fruit for a hundred years, are regarded as highly fertile trees.

Australian aborigines ate the phallic stinkhorn fungus in the belief that it would give them erections — however, its smell is pretty appalling, so the neighbours might complain. Far more

25

preferable would be a pittosporum tree — Aboriginal men are believed to have crushed the seeds and placed them near the shelters of their women, for the powerful aroma was said to drive them crazy with desire . . . if that failed, they would smear their chests with a paste made of fairy pantbrush bark and charcoal, believing its scent to have an instantaneous aphrodisiac effect. Interestingly, the Australian leafless mistletoe was once regarded as a love-inducing plant, in much the same way as its European cousin was.

FLOWERS — LOVE'S
TRUE LANGUAGE

Posies of particular flowers and flowered Valentine cards have
spoken volumes to initiates of the language of flowers for
many years. The original simple meanings became a well-
developed language for Victorian lovers, who were otherwise
inhibited by social mores and had to keep their true feelings
and actions hidden.

Even the way in which a gift of flowers was presented or
worn had its own particular cipher. For instance, if the answer
to a question was sought in the gift of a flower, passing it with
the right hand meant 'yes', the left 'no'. Messages could also
be read from where a gift of flowers was worn — if a girl wore
flowers in her hair, she was warning her suitor to be careful.
He could rejoice, however, if she placed the posy over her
heart, for she was giving him a clear signal that his love was
returned.

The same variety of flower will most often have different
meanings due to its different colours. Jasmine, for instance —
white means amiability; cape, transport to joy; Carolina says
"I hate this separation" and yellow pays tribute to the
recipient's grace and elegance. A red tulip signifies a heart
burning with love like a flame, although a yellow one meant
the affair was hopeless. Different varieties of daisies also say
different things — a garden daisy says "I share your feelings";
an ox-eye was a token of esteem; the white daisy meant
innocence, while the wild daisy signalled "I will think about
what you have said".

Chrysanthemums cover many aspects of lovers' language.
The red stands for true love, yellow means "I am affronted by

your manner" and a white one, like many white flowers, demands a truthful answer. The Chinese say that if you take a chrysanthemum to the table with you and use it to wipe your lips after having drunk some wine, you should give the flower to your lover as a token, for it will ensure his undying love and fidelity, being a symbol of eternal life.

Different cultures will ascribe widely varying meanings to the same flower. For instance, arum lilies, as a symbol of virginity, are a tribute to a woman's purity and mean the recipient is loved and respected. Similarly, it is very unlucky for a man to destroy a lily, as this will threaten the female members of his family. These meanings are far more refined than in the past when, due to its resemblance to the male sex organs, it was believed to be an aphrodisiac. Robust medieval country humour led to some dubious names for members of the lily family, "Lords and Ladies" and "Lady's Smock" being two used by folk contemplating such flowers in a 16th century mood. "Smock" had a double meaning, much as "skirt" does today, and "cuckoo" was synonymous with "cuckold" — thus making "cuckoo pint" or "cuckoo flower" an unwelcome inclusion in a bridal garland.

Another example is the peony. The prudish Victorians condemned it, saying that its rosy hues were the fiery cheeks of guilt as the flower had been the hiding place of a dis-honourable nymph. The Irish, however, loved them, as did the Chinese, who took the flower to signify fidelity and longevity due to its ability to live for more than 50 years. In fact, during the T'ang dynasty they were placed under the Emperor's protection. Being so esteemed, they were ex-changed as dowries and figured heavily in fabrics designed for bridal garments.

Flowers often owe their symbolic meanings to romantic — and sometimes tragic — histories. For instance the acanthus flower, though rarely offered as a gift, was favoured by Helen of Troy as a motif for her robes. It is said that a young Greek girl died in the 5th century B.C., and her nurse put her unused bride's bouquet and veil into a basket near the grave, covering it with a tile. By the following spring, the leaves of an acanthus had grown around the basket and up as far as the tile. The Greek sculptor and architect Callimachus, on seeing this, immortalised the sight as the Corinthian column design.

Ancient tradition suggests that red carnations sprang from the grave of lovers, meaning 'alas, my poor heart'; a striped one meant the suit was refused, and a yellow one communicated disdain. More recently, it has become a Christian symbol of betrothal, marriage and eternal love. The Victorians named the carnation pink to be the foundation of love, as endorsed by Robbie Burns, who wrote of his wife:

"And I will pick the pink to be the emblem of my dear
For she's the pink of womankind, and blooms without a par."

English country folk named it the 'gillyflower' and maids used the juice as a sweet, clove-scented perfume. The petals were also soaked in wine to distil the clove flavour and used as an aphrodisiac and tonic.

Although a flower of romance, with Tennyson referring to:

". . . the sweet forget-me-not that grows for happy lovers . . ."

the origin of the flower's name was not a happy one. It was said that a young Austrian girl was walking along the Danube with her fiancé the evening before her marriage when she saw the deep blue flower bobbing on a wave. Pettishly, she demanded her lover jump in and obtain it for her — this he did, only to drown in the process, crying out to her "Lover, love me! Forget me not!"

A lovely flower to behold, the many-petalled ornamental dahlia is, however, most often used as a symbol of treachery and danger. This meaning was ascribed in fairly recent times — the Empress Josephine was enamoured of dahlias, and grew many varieties at the fabulous Malmaison. One of her ladies-in-waiting begged her lover — a gardener there — to steal some of the flower roots so she could also grow them. On

29

hearing of this, Josephine flew into a rage and had the pair of them flogged and jailed and — and even worse — destroyed over a hundred species of her stock of flowers when she spitefully set fire to the gardener's greenhouse.

Bachelor's buttons, or cornflowers, derived their Latin name from Cyanus, a rather mournful youth who spent much of his time making wreaths of the bright blue flowers as tributes to Flora, the goddess of the flowers. While their colour remained fresh, the recipient had time to change her mind; however, as they faded, so would the giver's affections.

Anemone, or 'daughter of the wind' was, in Classical mythology, a nymph beloved of Zephyr. This aroused the anger of Flora, who turned her into a flower which always blooms just before the Northern spring. Zephyr abandoned the luckless girl to Boreas, the harsh north wind, who always disturbs her emotions so that she blooms too early, is bruised and dies. If, in a fit of pique, a posy of anemones is sent, it is a none-too-subtle wish that the recipient has a short, unhappy future.

Asters and michaelmas daisies were both once laid on the graves of war-dead in France to symbolise after-thought and a wish that things might have worked out differently. Peri-winkles were the traditional flowers of death and sorrow, used as mock crowns for condemned criminals on their way to the gallows. Culpeper, however, would contradict this. He tells us that 'the leaves of periwinkle eaten by man and wife together does cause love between them' and would probably see it as an inappropriate choice for an unlucky suitor.

The tuberose, so rich in appearance and scent, was a sure sign of mutual affection if received from the hands of a lady. In the East, the meaning was similar, and Tom Moore referred to:

> ". . . the tuberose with her silvery light
> that in the gardens of Malay
> is called the Mistress of the Night."

A young man could plead his case with a wistful tribute of willow, telling of his pain. Much associated with those who

have been jilted in love, it used to be believed that if a person
had been forsaken, he should wear willow leaves on his breast
— the 'heart' of the tree, which was so used to grieving, would
then take on the pain. Deserted lovers were said to 'wear the
green willow' and Shakespeare used the theme of forsaken
love with most dramatic force when the poor Desdemona
sang before she was murdered for supposed adultery:

> "The poor soul lay sighing by a sycamore tree
> sing all a green willow
> Her salt tears fell from her and softened the stones
> sing willow, willow, willow."

In Wales, it was the custom at one time to send a willow
garland to a jilted girl or young man on the eve of the former
sweetheart's wedding to someone else as an unkind reminder
of happiness that could never be theirs.

> "Lavender blue, dilly-dilly,
> Lavender green,
> When I am king, dilly-dilly,
> You'll be my queen."

The fragrance of this pretty flower will still often waft from a
hope chest where a young girl has tenderly tucked a lavender
sachet amongst her linens and lawns; as Scott observed so
sweetly — ". . . even the old maid (has) her little romance
carefully preserved in the lavender of memory." However, on
a more bawdy note, one of the Elizabethan poets, Robert
Greene, has a character advise his son that to win his lady love
he should hide in her chest so that "she may lay thee up in
lavender and . . . put thee on"!

Surprisingly, lavender symbolises distrust, danger or
caution. This is based on the legend that the asp which
poisoned Cleopatra lived behind a lavender bush. The early
Greeks didn't do much for lavender's reputation, either,
favouring this flower to deck their virgin victims before
sacrificing them to savage gods. Greek men in later times had a

far more pragmatic reason for disliking the scent of lavender, however — its price. Martial, in his Epigrams complains that his pretty young mistress has greedily demanded from him either ". . . a pound of nard (lavender essence)" or a "like-priced pair of sardonyxes" and wonders whether the girl is worth his trouble and money.

Narcissus was the shepherd of Classical mythology who died in a delirium of self-love while searching for his own image in a pool; the flower therefore symbolised egotism and conceit. The pretty border-flowers of campanula had a similar meaning. Also known as "Venus' Looking Glass", the story goes that Venus dropped one of her hand-mirrors to earth by mistake. A shepherd picked it up and, finding the reflection of himself more beautiful than he really was, fell in love with it. His rejected mistress complained to Cupid who obliged by breaking the mirror into a thousand pieces — which became the shining azure flowers.

Foxgloves, in the language of flowers, mean insincerity and trickery. This probably is due to the use of foxglove juice by the fairies when they exchanged unwanted changelings with human babies. Foxgloves possess great power and can be used for good and evil — it is said that the fairies gave the flowers to foxes to use as gloves on their paws, so they could travel in absolute silence.

The tiny sweet violet was much used by Shakespeare in his work as a symbol of constancy and faithfulness. A pretty Victorian valentine poem states:

> "A violet breath, that opes with magic key
> The inmost chambers of my heart,
> And sets its sweetest mem'ries free."

Napoleon was probably history's most famous violet devotee — when he married his Josephine, she wore violets and, on every wedding anniversary, he sent her a posy of them. When he was defeated and leaving for his final exile in St. Helena, he asked to visit her tomb; there, he picked violets and these were found in a locket around his neck when he died.

A bouquet of tulips signified perfect love that would survive the grave. A Persian legend tells us that the flower sprang from the blood of Prince Farhad, who flung himself off a mountain cliff when he learned that his beloved wife, Shirin, had died.

An unusual alternative, which would have a similar meaning, would be the zestily-perfumed lime blossom. This flower also came to symbolise conjugal love beyond the grave when Philemon and Baucis asked Zeus not to separate them in death — so, he turned them into a pair of lime trees.

Of course, not all gifts of flowers pass solely between men and women. Should two young men have a fondness for each other, a tribute of hyacinths would be in order. Hyacinthus was a handsome lad, beloved of the god Apollo. One day, when they were playing a game of quoits, Apollo unwittingly threw a quoit at Hyacinthus, and it killed him. He was heartbroken when he realised he would never see his companion again, so he changed him into the beautiful — and undeniably phallic — royal-hued flower.

Many cultures ascribe aspects of the rose's history to their own love goddesses. The rose was sacred to Venus, who was notorious for her affairs, and her shrines were showered with them, while in Hindu mythology the beautiful Sri, consort of Vishnu, was said to have been born in the heart of a rose. In Germany, the primitive earth goddess, Nerthus, was worshipped in rose groves, the sharp thorns protecting her sanctuaries. The cult of the rose traversed the chasm between paganism and Christianity, being adopted as the symbol for the mother of Christ — hence, the creation of fabulous, stained-glass 'rose' windows in cathedrals.

Amorous stories have grown around red roses. A Persian legend relates that the rose was white until the nightingale, in a frenzy of passion for its loveliness, pressed its breast against the rose until the thorns pierced its heart, staining the petals red. Another story claims that the roses blushed with shame when Adam and Eve were driven out of the Garden of Eden.

"Oh, my luve is like a red, red rose! That's newly sprung in June" wrote the poet, Robbie Burns. Red roses are much loved by romantics, for it is said that their blush bloomed from the blood of Aphrodite. Attempting to save her beloved Adonis from being attacked by a wild boar, she scrambled through a tangled white briar rose — blood from her feet stained the flowers, giving birth to the first red rose.

Other legends tell of star-crossed lovers — most notably Tristram and Isolde — dead untimely and buried near each other, upon whose graves red and white rose briars have sprung up, growing towards each other and becoming entwined in proof of the undying fidelity of those who slept beneath them. The old English ballad of "Sweet William and Fair Margaret" tells a similar tale:

"Out of her breast there sprang a rose
And out of his a briar
They grew and they grew till they reached the church top
And then, they could go no higher
So there they tied in a true lovers' knot
Which made all the people admire."

The yellow rose, however, has come to mean 'my love decreases', or 'I am jealous', being the flower of infidelity. Legend has it that the prophet Mohammed, suspecting that his favourite wife Aisha was being unfaithful to him, asked the archangel Gabriel what he should do. The archangel said that Mohammed must ask her to dip a bunch of red roses into the sacred river and see what happened. To her astonishment — and his righteous anger — the rose petals turned bright yellow.

Thinking of 'saying it with flowers' to your lover? Well, consider all or some of the following, to succinctly communicate just about anything you wish to say . . .

Oleander	Beware other's interference in our affair
Quince blossom	I will forswear all others to be with you always
Ranunculus	You dazzle me with your charms

34

Iris	Named for the glorious goddess of rainbows, this flower represents many blessings flowing from heaven to earth
Lotus	Our present estrangement makes me sad, but I think we should remain apart
Mistletoe	I am determined to overcome difficulties in this life; if it cannot be as we wish, we will meet in the next world
Daisy	You have as many virtues as this plant has petals; I will think about your request
Petunia	We must bravely face the despair caused by our separation
Split reed	Be careful — others are aware of our indiscretion
Buttercup	You are immature, a heartless and ungrateful flirt
Primroses	Your inconsistency saddens me
Love-in-the-mist	I am perplexed by your behaviour. What is it you want?
Columbines	Oh, your folly!
Hydrangeas	You are too cool and proud for my taste, a coquette
Pansies	From the French 'pensée' for 'thoughts'. I think only of your sweet face
Almond blossom	I hope to meet you again
American linden	Can we not wed soon? Matrimony would be such bliss!
Ivy	We shall cling together in the spirit of fidelity and lasting friendship — nothing will separate us.
Chestnut leaves	Please be just and fair in your dealings
Christmas rose	I beg you to relieve my anxiety
Clover flowers	Think carefully about what I have said
Geranium	I miss you so, please comfort me

Heather	We shall be lucky in our life together
Gorse	I offer you my enduring affection
Myrtle	Joyously do I return your love
Everlasting peas	I long for a tryst
Speedwell	You are a true and faithful woman
Jonquils	Your affection is returned, fondly
Forget-me-not	Here is the key to my heart
Strawberry plant	I esteem you as a friend, but not as a lover
Snowdrop	Please accept my consolation; I wish you well for the future
Lily of the valley	Worry not, happiness will return
Sweetpeas	Only in your departure will I find any pleasure
Pennyroyal	Leave me quickly
Burdock	(also known as 'Touch Me Not') — your suit is emphatically rejected
Chaste tree	Coldness and indifference; I prefer to remain a virgin than to let you come near me
Daffodil	My fond hopes have been dashed by your behaviour
Candytuft	I am indifferent to you and your wiles
Love-lies-bleeding	All hope of love is lost for you and me
Magnolia	Although you have broken my heart, I shall persevere with dignity
Mignonette	Your charms and qualities surpass all before
Heliotrope	I am so devoted to you
Angelica	You are my perfect inspiration
Queen asters	You are so dainty
Peach blossom	I am your captive
Cowslips	Your grace and beauty have charmed me completely
Asphodel	My regrets follow you to the grave

SETTING A SEXY TABLE

Planning a lusty dinner à deux? The love-starved masses have often experimented with conventional foods in an unconventional way. For instance, fruits, vegetables and nuts have been considered aphrodisiacs — containing the very seeds of life, this is not altogether surprising. For the same reason, they play a prominent part in wedding ceremonies around the world.

Fruit

The ancients believed that the fertility of the tree would be passed on to whoever ate the tree's first fruit, with the first offender traditionally being the apple:

> "And the woman saw that the tree was good to eat, and fair to the eye, and delightful to behold; and she took of the fruit thereof and did eat and gave to her husband, who did eat."

The first thing that Adam and Eve did after tasting this forbidden fruit was to roll and tumble amongst the flowers. Due to their lustful behaviour, the apple became an aphrodisiac of the highest quality.

In countries where it is a native, the orange tree has been regarded for many centuries as a fruitful plant, of which both the flowers and fruit were used in love and fertility charms:

> "Suzanne takes you down, to a place by the river
> And she feeds you tea and oranges, that come all the way from
> China . . ."
>
> Leonard Cohen

The Stuart kings first popularised orange blossom as a wedding decoration, instead of the myrtle or rosemary hitherto used. English folklore suggests that you may obtain another's affections if you take an orange, prick it all over with a needle and then sleep with it in your left armpit. Give it to the object of your affections to eat, and he or she will become enamoured of you, also. A simpler charm to bring about love between a young boy and girl is for them to exchange oranges as gifts.

The peach, with its soft, suggestive cleavage, is a traditional symbol of female sexuality amongst the Chinese — Chinese brides are still called by a word that translates as 'peach'. Apricots and apricot flowers are used in cosmetics by Oriental women, and included in medicines to treat female ailments.

Jellied or pickled figs were served as a delicacy at Chinese wedding feasts. Japanese women similarly believe that figs create a fertile and happy atmosphere, so are quite likely to keep a potted fig tree near the main doorway to repel demons. The ancient Greeks, however, had a more down-to-earth view of figs. Believing the fruit's phallic shape referred to its prowess as an aphrodisiac, they reserved them for consumption at the lusty Dionysian orgies. Primitive cultures also believed bananas to be love food, because of their shape, while prunes were served to patrons of Elizabethan brothels to prepare them for their appointment.

The pomegranate tree, native to the East and Tropical Africa, is one of the oldest fertility symbols in the world, due to its prolific number of seeds. Pomegranate designs were carved on stone altars and around capitals of temple pillars, and they were served at important marriage and religious festivals to ensure love and fecundity.

"Behold, thou art fair my love . . .
Thy temples are like a piece of pomegranate within thy locks . . ."

Song of Solomon

The Greeks valued pomegranates, believing the seeds to have sprung from the blood of Dionysius, who passed on to the fruit his gifts of abundance and lusty abandonment. Sugared pomegranate seeds are served to guests at a Chinese wedding and, when the newly-weds enter their chamber, one is broken on the threshold — the bursting fruit strew their seeds all over the room, signifying that the marriage will be happy and blessed with many children.

The Aztec's name for avocado was 'ahuacatl', meaning 'testicle'. The conquering Spanish were convinced by the natives of the fruit's merits in promoting passion, and introduced it to the courts of Europe as one of the treasures of the New World. Even today, nutritionists substantiate avocado's claims as an aphrodisiac by citing its rich protein content, although most of us would agree its value comes from its seductive and exotically rich smoothness of texture — a suggestiveness that cannot be ignored.

The delicate fruit of the mulberry tree is said to be a food for true lovers, though its story is a sad one. According to Ovid, Pyramus and Thisbe were two young people in love who were forbidden to marry. They arranged a rendezvous and when Thisbe arrived, she was terrified by the sight of a lion eating an ox. She fled, leaving the lion to paw at her cloak, which she dropped in her haste. When Pyramus arrived and found the blood-stained cloak, he presumed she was dead, and, heart-broken, he killed himself beneath a mulberry tree. The blood from his broken heart is said to have coloured the berries.

However, not all berries augur well as love fruit. Mirroring a similar belief in Normandy, the people of Herefordshire in England avoid blackberries and consider their presence in a garden or near a house to be an ill omen for the happiness of the couple within. This is because, according to the fable, the Devil once tripped in a blackberry thicket and scratched himself badly. So angry was he that he spat on the tree and cursed it — the glossy berries are said to have formed from his spittle.

Vegetables

The word 'vegetable' comes from the Latin 'vegetus', meaning to be active and lively. The vegetable kingdom can claim many foods which are often incorporated in fertility and marriage rituals. For instance, in Europe, peas are still tossed at a newly wed couple to ensure they have many children, and the custom of showering the bride with rice — taking particular care to aim some straight at her neckline, so it falls inside her dress — is well-nigh universal.

Carrots were once prized as a food to be served before amatory affairs. Its phallic shape gave it a reputation as a powerful passion agent — the Greeks were so enamoured of it that they named it 'philtron', meaning 'to love'. Arabian princesses served carrots spiced with cardamom and cooked in milk to enhance their effect, while John Gerard mentions the wild variety as 'serving well for love matters'. Old wives would prescribe quantities of boiled carrots for nervous youths — interestingly, carrots do have certain constituents which help relieve bronchial congestion, so could have emboldened a wheezy lad who had trouble talking to a pretty lass.

Asparagus has long been respected as an erotic delicacy. Nicolas Culpeper recommended boiling the stalks till soft, and eating them for three mornings running to "... stirreth up bodily luste in man and woman, whatever some may have written to the contrary." Beans were another vegetable regarded as a potent love food during this period, as evidenced by this risqué Elizabethan drinking song:

> "My love hung limp beneath the leaf
> (O bitter, bitter shame!)
> My heavy heart was full of grief
> Until my lady came
>
> She bought a tasty dish to me
> (O swollen pod, and springing seed!)
> My love sprang out right eagerly
> To serve me in my need."

Various vegetables have earned a place in love lore for reasons other than their shape. Witness the success of Popeye — spinach was the secret of his strength when pursuing the lugubrious Olive Oyl. Another leafy vegetable of note is the lettuce. In some areas, it has been considered dangerous to women, as it was thought to promote barrenness, as noted by Sir Thomas Elyot (1539), who recommended a decoction made from the juice and seeds to actually "abateth carnall appetite." Similarly, Beatrix Potter's "Flopsy Bunnies" were warned that 'eating too much lettuce is soporific'. The Romans, however, loved it, and eyed its inclusion in a banquet menu with great favour — for this meant that their host was supplying erotic games as part of the feast to come. In ancient Egypt, lettuce was considered to be a divine victual, and tomb-paintings show the mighty god-kings holding lettuces.

Not everyone would regard cabbages as particularly romantic. However, in France, "my little cabbage", or "mon petit chou" is a loving nickname and a large family, happy household and fine harvest are all the outcome of a crop of fine fat cabbages in a Provence market garden.

Possibly the aphrodisiac properties of tomatoes could be ascribed to the fact that they are rich in potassium, which vitalises the body and stimulates the nervous system. At any rate, they were called 'love apples' or 'pommes d'amour'. In the 16th century, even the humble potato was said to be a powerful love charm, and they were sold to gullible folk for £250 per pound!

When eaten in large quantities, radishes and pimento are two vegetables which stimulate and irritate the bladder — the source of their aphrodisiac reputation — and the truffle has been lauded as a love food by those who should know, including Madame du Barry and the Marquis de Sade.

Onions, or 'ciswadi' are an important element in love rites of South African natives. The dried skin is — quite sensibly, given its antiseptic properties — used as a healing wrap for the penis after circumcision. They are also eaten by the bride and groom as they sing a wedding song and, in Europe, were said to increase sperm. A young girl can also use whole, fat onions in love divination particularly when deciding between several lovers. She should scratch the name of each suitor on a separate onion, then put all of them away in a cool, dark place. The onion which sprouts first is the preferred option. To bring about a vision of the husband-to-be a girl could stick nine pins in a brown onion on St. Thomas' Eve, while reciting:

> "Good St. Thomas, do me right
> Send me my true love this night."

Bread

Breads are strongly associated with erotic love because of their historical association with phallic worship. Breads and cakes, baked in male and female shapes, were prepared by the ancient Greek and Roman prostitutes, who were called 'bakers' girls', and in early Christian times, phallic loaves were baked on holy days and carried in religious processions until the church frowned on the custom and ordered bread to be baked in less inflammatory shapes.

> "A loaf of bread, and thou beside me
> beneath the bough
> were Paradise enow."

The various grains used through the ages to bake cakes, pastries or bread have fascinating individual histories as love and fertility stimulants. For instance, maize was considered a god by the Mayan and Inca Indian tribes of South America, and they honoured it with special sowing dances and prayers and festivals of thanks with human sacrifices at harvest time.

In the East, rice was revered as a symbol of fertility and the custom of showering it over newly-weds originated at Oriental weddings. The Indonesians, who regard the rice plant as a living being with a beneficent soul, go one step further. They will fashion a male and female doll from the cuttings of the plant and, accompanied by prayer and ritual, place them on an altar shaped to resemble a sleeping-couch, and leave them undisturbed. These two rice spirits are then believed to unite and their offspring is a healthy crop for the village.

Wheat, corn and barley are the crops most frequently found in western farming communities. Wheat is today regarded as a rich source of Vitamin E, "the fertility vitamin", and lack of vitamin E has shown to result in sterility and lack of vitality.

As with all grains, many rituals were employed to bring about a fine wheat harvest, and girls would capitalise on the fertile atmosphere with a love charm for themselves. For instance, a European farmer's daughter would jump naked into a tub of unground wheat and rub herself all over with it. She would then take a handful of this grain and pound it into a special biscuit to offer to the man of her choice. He was said to be unable to resist the charms of the baker and would ask her to marry him immediately.

The success of the corn crop was long linked with man's ability to reproduce, given the vegetable's phallic shape. In Europe, many harvest customs have an obvious reference to marriage and childbirth, and nearly all stemmed from the ritual worshipping of the Earth Mother, Ceres, pagan goddess of all that grows, for she was believed to live in the corn fields. From this belief grew the traditional use of 'corn dollies' — most common in England, where the farmer's wife will preserve the last stalks of corn from a field and bind them into the shape of a woman. This 'dolly' is then displayed on the farmhouse wall during harvest festivities to ensure a good crop and fortuitous year to follow. In Brittany, the last sheaf of corn is carefully shaped to resemble a woman and a smaller 'baby' sheaf is placed inside it. The Bretons believe that whoever is presented with the dolly will be pregnant before the end of the year.

Until relatively recently, men and women were sent to frolic on the newly-planted soil, in order to show the seeds exactly what they had to do. In Russia, these proceedings were blessed by the local priest and, in the Ukraine, the men of God were expected to overcome any personal squeamishness and take part in the proceedings — for additional spiritual impetus, so to speak. In Central South Africa, it was a strict religious duty for the couple to have sex just as the seed was sown and, in Borneo, the farmer and his wife had to visit each field on consecutive nights for the same purpose.

Wine

A charming story, concerning the first production of wine, is as follows: the Arabian prince Jemshed, being very fond of grape juice, stored a number of goatskin bags of it in the cellar of his desert palace. After a time, it began to ferment and tasted foul, giving him a severe stomach-ache. To stop others from drinking it, he labelled all the bags 'poison'. A short time later, one of his wives who had fallen from the prince's favour decided to kill herself by drinking glass after glass of the 'poison'. Instead of dying, however, she found she became much happier and, with her glowing skin and intoxicated hilarity, she regained the prince's love. When the prince found the goat-skins to be empty, she told him what had happened, and he became the first wine-maker.

Certainly, this story gives credence to the long-touted aphrodisiac qualities of alcohol, for it has been successfully used for this purpose since the Greek deities drank 'nectar of the gods' on Mount Olympus during their revels. This stimulating, mysterious and highly potent beverage, made from wine, ambrosia and thyme blossoms, and the orgiastic rites preceding its use, were supervised by the louche god, Dionysius. The Romans changed his name to Bacchus later on, and continued to hold drunken escapades in his honour. Best of all, they loved champagne and would gather at mixed baths to shed their togas and leap with abandon into a pool of bubbly. Another favourite of the decadent Romans was rose or violet wine, made by infusing petals for a week, then sweetening the liquid with honey and serving in be-flowered cups.

In his dotage, Louis XIV yearned for the excesses of his youth and drank special wine-based cordials and liqueurs, containing vanilla, cinnamon and brandy, for their stimulating effect on his slumbering amatory instincts. These sound, no doubt, like warming tonics, but too much of any strong drink ruins its potential aphrodisiac effect, as Shakespeare's porter in 'Macbeth' knew well. He summed up the relative merits — and demerits — of alcohol as an aphrodisiac:

Macduff: What three things does drink especially provoke?
Porter: Marry sir, nose-painting, sleep and urine.
             Lechery, sir, it provoke and unprovokes. It
             provokes the desire, but takes away the per-
             formance . . . it persuades him and disheartens
             him, makes him stand to and not stand to . . .
             equivocates him in a sleep and, giving him the
             lie, leaves him.

The abuse and over-use of alcohol in the uplifting of a man's desire and a girl's skirt, can as the porter pointed out, dampen performance indeed. Alcohol's power as a stimulant to passion is well known, but it must be treated with care. Caddish seducers may, therefore, be interested to learn that 3 drops of fermented cyclamen juice, when added to a girl's glass of wine, triples its effect. So, even if she only takes a moderate amount, she will quickly become intoxicated. Lord Byron is believed to have employed this method when preying on unsuspecting women, immortalising the result in 'Don Juan':

> "A little she strove, and much repented
> And whispering 'I'll ne'er consent'
> — consented."

Seafood

Art and mythology have contributed strongly to the marriage of seafood and love-food. Aphrodite herself was born of the sea when Cronus castrated his father and threw his genitals into the sea. The foam, being thus fertilised, gave birth to the lovely goddess and she rose from the waves to ride to shore in a scallop-shell blown by the west wind. A dual personality, inspiring both the purest ideal love and prostitution, she is often pictured with a swan or goose, a phallic symbol of the god Priapus.

In Roman times Aphrodite's equivalent, Venus, was depicted with her legs astride a tortoise — the extended head and neck also being a phallic symbol.

> "In Venice, why so many whores abound?
> The reason sure is easy to be found,
> Because as sages all agree
> Fair Venus' birthplace was the salt, salt sea."
>
> Traditional

It is therefore interesting that tortoise flesh and tortoise soup are highly prized among Oriental cultures for their ability to inflame the passions, as is shark's fin soup. Most efficacious of all is bird's nest soup, made from the nests of sea-swallows and edible seaweed, with the added frisson of fish spawn.

Fish themselves are rich in valuable minerals and trace elements, such as iodine and phosphorus — both of these substances favour the reproductive system.

> "Old impotent Alden from Walden
> Ate salmon to heat him to scaldin'
> 'Twas just the ticket
> To stiffen his wicket
> This salmon of Amorous Alden"
>
> Anonymous

Friday is the traditional day for Christians to eat fish — one wonders whether this was originally because it was the day sacred to Freya, the Norse goddess of love. Like her Greek and Roman counterparts, Freya was ocean-born and granted fertility to barren women. Fish are also very prolific — they lay enormous numbers of eggs so fish roe, such as caviar, is highly recommended as a delicacy and as an aphrodisiac.

Oysters are among the best-known of all folklore love foods, though nobody seems to know exactly why. Along with caviar, they are usually quite expensive, although this was not always the case. In fact, they were once so much a food of the working class that Dickens had one of his characters say- "... poverty and oysters always go together. The poorer a place is, the greater the call there seems to be for oysters". Still, the mere mention of the word 'aphrodisiac' will conjure up visions of oysters in most lascivious minds. They should be eaten raw for maximum potency.

Ancient Romans believed many other shellfish to be especially invigorating and they frequently added zest to their libidinous appetites with crab, lobsters and mussels. Recipes featuring octopus, eel and squid are often employed by enterprising Lotharios, and even the humble anchovy was much favoured by the Victorians who, with their passion for sauces and essences, enjoyed their salty, stimulating taste.

Sweetmeats

Ernst Gombrich wrote that "... for the historian, the chocolate box is one of the most significant products of our age — precisely because of its role as a catalyst." The modern custom of giving a box of chocolates to a loved one had its beginnings in the ancient belief in the aphrodisiac properties of sweetmeats.

Many aphrodisiacs act as stimulants, but honey is also invaluable as one of the best and quickest forms of energy. It is the most easily absorbed form of sugar and has other advantages as an aphrodisiac, being a mine of all sorts of vitamins, minerals and trace elements. In the Song of Solomon, the enamoured bridegroom gave sweet tribute to his bride, saying:

"Thy lips, my spouse, are as dropping honeycomb: honey and milk are under thy tongue and the smell of thy garments is as the smell of frankincense."

It is no accident that in Arabia, the legendary land of sexual prowess, sweetmeats were always made from spiced honey. Even the word 'honeymoon' was so named from the ancient Teutonic custom of drinking honey-wine, or hydromel, for the first thirty days after marriage. Attila the Hun over-indulged in hydromel at his own nuptials — he drank so much of it, that he died.

Two famous physicians — Galen, a 2nd century Greek and Avicenna, a 13th century Arab — both recommended honey for affairs of the heart. The Hindus also regard honey as a powerful love nectar and serve honey-based sweets at the end of a big meal. As honey counteracts the effects of alcohol, such a practice could well give a guest renewed energy.

In the Orient, honey is a common substitute for sugar and often appears in love recipes. Chinese honey (mi tang) is still used today as a binding agent in aphrodisiac pills concocted by Hong Kong apothecaries. Another product from the bee, pollen, while not a sweetmeat has also been regarded as an aphrodisiac. Pills containing pollen have claimed great success in curing various sexual problems, including impotence, in East Germany and Denmark.

In the 15th and 16th centuries, sweet 'confects' or 'comfits' were used as household medicines and the confection box played the part our medicine chest plays today. A well-stocked confection box contained different types of sugary pastilles, made from seeds, spices and herbs, mixed with honey and saffron. Almond, aniseed and powdered cherry stones were administered to stimulate the milk supply of nursing mothers and reduce labour pain. Brandied cubeb berries were used to prevent venereal disease; ginger and nutmeg were used as breath sweeteners, giving rise to the generic name of 'kissing comfits', popularised during the Elizabethan era and remaining in use till Victorian times.

Violets and rose petals candied in caster sugar were first made popular in Italy as love-provoking sweetmeats, before taking the English Tudor court by storm. Dioscorides was actually the first to ascribe aphrodisiac properties to sweet-tasting flowers or their parts, namely tulip seeds, and both Gerard and Parkinson went on to recommend their tonic properties. Chopped and jellied, tulip roots had been popular long before the phrase 'kissing comfit' was coined. In ancient Constantinople, the Sultan was wont to hold an annual banquet in his seraglio, called the Feast of the Tulips. Here, his guests would eat the jellied root with a ginger sauce and enjoy the spectacle of the Sultan's gardens illuminated to show tulips of every colour. Similarly, the root of the opium poppy was crystallised and served with wine as a narcotic and aphrodisiac in Assyria and Babylon.

The Ladies Dictionary warned in 1649 that ". . . eryngoes are not good for to be taken and, with lust-provoking meats must be forsaken." Eryngo root, from the sea-holly plant, was a popular aphrodisiac. Sixteenth century apothecaries recommended a drink comprising egg yolks beaten with Madeira, to which eryngoes and ambergris had been added, as a tonic to restore the 'vital force' in men who were no longer young. Candied sweetmeats were made from them and sold in the streets in the days of Charles II and there are many references to them in the work of the Restoration poets. So great was the demand for eryngo sweets during the 18th century that a whole factory was set up for them in Colchester, England.

Of course, no discussion of erotic sweets would be complete without mentioning one of the world's most divine flavours — chocolate. The Aztecs first discovered it and found it stimulating, drinking it in honour of Xochiquetzal, their goddess of love. Even Linnaeus, the very dry and pragmatic scientist, named the chocolate tree "theobromia", meaning "food for the gods", for it was so delicious.

Having been introduced to Europe, hot chocolate rapidly assumed such erotic popularity that both young women and monks were forbidden to drink it, lest it tempt them to the sins of the flesh. At the same time, lascivious matrons across the countryside almost exhausted supplies, believing it to make them irresistible to young men.

In the licentious French courts of Louis XIV, chocolates

were dipped in ambergris and sent as a gift to a potential mistress. If she popped one in her mouth in view of the king, it signified that she accepted his 'invitation'. Following this Gallic tradition, Napoleon developed a personal recipe for a drink combining equal parts of chocolate, musk and coffee, which is still advocated in France as a strengthening potion and fed to elderly gentlemen — presumably the high sugar content helps to feed sagging energy levels.

By the 17th century, European gentlefolk had put vanilla and chocolate together, regarding the joint taste as a pure aphrodisiac. The French regarded the Bourbon vanilla pod as the best, adding it to cream and ices as well as chocolate. Vanilla also owed part of its stimulating reputation to its appearance — the bean being regarded as a female symbol.

The Aztecs were again the first to use vanilla as a love spice for centuries, although it was not until the invasion by Cortes in 1520 that Europe learned about it. It is said that a conquistadore observing the Emperor Montezuma eating foods laced with the vanilla bean's essence, imperiously demanded that he also be allowed to sample this taste of the gods. Delighted with it, he took some plants of the vanilla orchid back to Europe. However, Montezuma cursed the surly conquistadore by ensuring that only certain types of Mexican bees and hummingbirds could fertilise the plant, thus ensuring that Mexico remained the sole supplier of vanilla to the world for many years to come.

Vanilla does have invigorating and tonic properties, as do many other members of the orchid family; and herbalists today still use orchids as a remedy for ovarian and uterine disorders. In fact, they originally went by the name of Satyrions as, in mythology, the orchid flower was said to have been born from the blood of a wanton satyr who was killed for raping a Bacchanalian priestess. The name Satyrion was, therefore, derived from the fable that this plant was the food of the satyr and brought about their erotic behaviour.

Another orchid favoured in the preparation of aphrodisiacs and stimulants was Lady's Slipper. These were made into a sweet paste called 'salop', which was the main ingredient in nearly every 'poculum amatorium' in the 17th and 18th centuries. There was even a 'salop house' at one time in Fleet Street in London. Sassafras was the other major ingredient in salop. The roots of this plant were brought from North America to England by Sir Francis Drake. Later, when the Spanish and French mercenaries returning from America brought the new knowledge that sassafras was a cure for syphilis, the public imbibing of the beverage lost its popularity.

Two of the most common flavours found in a box of chocolates are peppermint and hazelnut, both of which have histories steeped in love lore.

Mint was named by the unwilling Queen of Hades, Persephone. When she found her husband was in love with the nymph Menthe, she changed her into a plant whose leaves combined the coldness of betrayal and the warmth of passion. Most noticeable in spearmint and peppermint, it is this coolness that provides aphrodisiac properties, providing an excellent balance to hot or rich foods, and toning up the passions on a hot summer's day.

Shakespeare suggested that "hot lavender, mints, savory and marjoram" be given to "men of middle age" as an aphrodisiac tonic; in modern times there is even an American superstitition which claims that a boy can win a girls' affections by giving her a piece of spearmint chewing gum — provided he has made a wish over it prior to this.

Since Victorian times, nuts have symbolised fertility and new life; in particular, hazel nuts were given in the spirit of a loving request for reconciliation after a lovers' tiff. This was probably a result of ancient Irish and English folk beliefs. Historically in Ireland, the hazel was the tree of wisdom, whose nuts dropped into the water and fed the sacred salmon; in England, hazel nuts were associated with fertility and in many countries still, a plentiful crop of nuts in any parish is said to foretell numerous births there in the coming year. "Good nutting year, plenty boy babies" is a well-known country saying, to which is sometimes added that if the tree bore an unusually large crop of double nuts, a correspondingly large number of twins was expected.

The phrase "going a-nutting" once meant love-making and English expeditions to gather hazel-nuts were quite licentious revels. The Devil himself is associated with hazel nuts in English tradition and girls who went gathering nuts on Sundays were said to meet him in the woods where he would bend branches down to help them pick the nuts. On Holy Rood Day (September 14), when young people used to go nutting in bands, there was always a risk that he might attach himself to their group, uninvited and frightening:

"The Devil, as the common people say
Doth go a-nutting on Holy Rood Day
And sure such lechery in some doth lurk
Going a-nutting, do the Devil's work."

CHARMS, GAMES AND OMENS

Child'sPlay

When children play or sing, they are unaware that they are continuing ancient traditions and games, many of which — despite female emancipation — concern their romantic future.

For example, accompanying the counting of cherry stones around one's plate with "Tinker, tailor, soldier, sailor, rich man, poor man, beggarman, thief" is a popular means of ascertaining a future husband's profession. A more modern version from America to accompany the buttoning up of a little girl's dress, has as its first line "A doctor, a lawyer, a merchant, a chief..." "This year, next year, sometime, never" determines the date she will wed, and whether she will be clothed in "silk, satin, muslin or rags".

Another method used by schoolgirls is to write down their own names and those of their boyfriends, crossing out those letters they have in common and counting the remainder while reciting — "Love, marriage, friendship, hate, adore."

Tickling games are of great antiquity and are still favoured by children today. Again, the importance of courtship and marriage is instilled early on with such rhymes as:

"Tickle, tickle on the knee
If you laugh, then you don't love me
If you're a lady, as I take you to be,
You'll neither laugh nor smile when I tickle your knee.
Old maid, old maid, you'll surely be
If you laugh or smile when I tickle your knee."

A game peculiar to young girls in Korea was called 'nul',

53

and involved bouncing each other high in the air on sprung boards or sticks. Some claim it was made popular long ago because it allowed a glimpse of possible suitors beyond the walls of the girls' secluded compounds. The ancient game of stone-throwing amongst boys may have had a similar heritage — often hundreds of men would gather to hurl rocks at designated targets, to demonstrate their strength and prowess to any female audience which may have been present.

In days of yore, children were more likely to manufacture their own toys and create their own amusement, often mimicking adult behaviour. Mother's vegetable garden may have been assaulted by schoolboys, if they were left unsupervised nearby. Originating in Scotland, the game of 'peascod-wooing' entailed a boy choosing a pod, tearing it off the stem as roughly and noisily as possible, then checking to see if the peas were still intact inside the pod. If they were, his crush on the girl of his choice was likely to prosper and he would present her with the pod as a gift. If he did not have any particular girl in mind, he could snap open more pods and count the peas inside to the spell "thin, pretty, fat or silly" and thus gain clues as to her appearance and nature.

Welsh boys and girls would be more likely to ransack the flower garden, pressing handfuls of cowslips into a large ball. This would then be tossed quickly from one to another, as they chanted:

> "Tisty tosty, tell me true
> Who will I be married to?"

On the last line, the child to whose lot it fell, had to juggle the ball while calling out the names of all the likely members of the opposite sex in the neighbourhood. The ball disintegrated when the right one was mentioned.

Little girls still pluck daisy petals while murmuring "He loves me, he loves me not" to find out their sweetheart's real intentions, a charming practice which gave rise to the old country name for the daisy — 'measure of love'. The dandelion can also serve as a love oracle, for if an unmarried girl plucks one fresh from the ground and blows the puffball of seeds, the number of puffs it takes to remove them all will indicate the number of years she will have to wait before her wedding.

Violets were another popular flower in children's mock-serious games, with their overtones of issues of life and love. A sweet charm for young or old involves joining two (using the 'hook' behind the flower head) and making a wish for a marriage partner who is as gentle as this flower as they are pulled apart.

Children have long made clover chains, by tying the stem of one flower around the head of another until it is long enough to make a fairy skipping rope, and laid on the grass. Little girls will jump blindfolded into such a ring and make a wish that the man they marry will be strong and good. Clover chains also make pretty necklaces, crowns and sashes when play-acting a wedding.

English children used acorn cups, much as gypsy fortune-tellers did. Placing a pea or small silver coin under one of three inverted cups, they would be shuffled on a table while the play-partner was not looking. Omens, such as the number of years before a wedding, would be drawn from the order in which the cups were selected.

Help from on High

As the girls and boys grew a little older, the question of their matrimonial future became of even more pressing interest, and they indulged in more serious methods of divining the future.

Help has been enlisted from On High since time immemorial. Holy books, such as the Bible, the Torah and the Koran, may be used to foresee the future and to resolve personal doubts and complexities, such as when a cautious young man seeks advice about a potential bride. To provide a clue to her nature and temperament, he would turn to the

Book of Proverbs in the Bible and read the verse whose number corresponded with her age.

A girl wishing to know if she would marry would place her door key in the 'Song of Solomon' section, leaving the key ring protruding. She then bound the Bible closed tightly, with her garter or stocking, and suspended it by the ring, while reciting:

> "Many waters cannot quench love, neither can the floods drown it. Love is as strong as death, but jealousy is as cruel as the grave. If a man should give all the substance of his house for love, it would all be utterly consumed."

Should the Bible turn or fall when these words are spoken, she will marry; if nothing happens, she will die unwed. The same charm could be used to find out the initials of the future partner. After the verse had been recited, the alphabet was said slowly while the book turned slowly on the garter-and-ring mechanism. When the prospective mate's initial was reached, the book would drop or spin faster; the entire exercise would be repeated to find out the initial of the surname.

Italian girls tended to make their appeals more direct, rather than go through the third party of the Bible. Before leaving the church after evening prayers, they would earnestly devote the following address to the Mother of Christ:

> "I take not oil for my affliction
> But take I the benediction
> From the hand of saint'd Maria
> To move the man to me so dear
> Mother, may he ne'er depart
> The safety of my tender heart."

Strangely Ordinary Omens

Sentimental girls were tireless in their search for omens, for the fear of remaining on the shelf was a very real one. Just about every item or occurrence that she would come across in the course of her day could provide a clue to her future — this way of looking at the world being heartily endorsed by Francis Bacon, who said "there is (nothing) that hath not some strangeness in its proportion".

A girl from Eastern Europe would be careful to look towards the north when she first left the house for the day; even a practical modern American woman would be wary of picking up a furled umbrella; and girls everywhere avoided reading the marriage ceremony to themselves — all to avoid the fate of being an old maid.

In the kitchen, if two teaspoons were accidentally placed in the one saucer, it indicated a wedding. A variant of this omen says that the two teaspoons mean the girl will marry twice. In Wales, young men used to carve elaborate wooden spoons, known as 'love spoons' and give them to the girl of their choice to hang in her kitchen as a token of their esteem.

A knife could be used to find out whether a future husband would be dark or fair. The enquirer would take a table-knife with a white haft and spin it on a table, noting the way it stopped. If it fell with the blade closest to the person, the future partner would be dark; if with the haft, they would be fair.

Aprons could mean a variety of things. A commonly held belief amongst English girls is that bad luck will eventuate if an apron suddenly falls off, although an Oxfordshire lass will take it to mean she will have a baby within the year. In Europe, a girl will say this means her lover is thinking of her. The apron also features in two German traditions — the first being that if a man wipes his hands on a girl's apron, he will fall in love with her. Once engaged or married, though, he must not do this, for it will result in a quarrel.

Needles have long been associated with matters of the heart. British tradition states that if a girl breaks a needle or pricks her finger while making a new dress, it is a sign she will be kissed while wearing it. A broken needle also portends a wedding, although it is unlucky to lend a whole one to replace it, as this will 'prick' the friendship.

The common pin has been the subject of much superstition for centuries, and was often used in love divination, as well as in charms to encourage good and repel evil.

> I'll give to you a paper of pins
> for that's the way my love begins
> If you will marry me, me, me
> If you will marry me.
>
> Traditional

A method for recalling a faithless or absent sweetheart was to throw twelve pins on the fire at midnight, while reciting the following:

> "'Tis no these pins I wish to burn
> but . . .'s heart I wish to turn
> May he neither sleep nor rest
> Till he has granted my request."

A woman from the English Midlands could torment an unfaithful husband simply by wearing nine pins concealed in her dress.

Pretty dressmakers would have spent many long hours sewing clothes by hand for their customers, hoping for a quick marriage as a way to end their drudgery — this perhaps explains the superstitions about pins held by that profession. For instance, if an unmarried dressmaker accidentally fastens the new dress to the customer's other clothes, the number of pins she uses in doing so will foretell the number of years before her own marriage. She would avoid picking up bent pins from the floor, because although it is lucky to pick up a straight pin:

> "See a pin, pick it up, all day long you'll have good luck"

a crooked one will ensure the woman never marries, remaining an old maid.

In Germany, the superstition still persists that if a young girl accidentally gets a pin stuck in her skirt, she will marry a man who has been married before. When girls do marry, it is very important for their attendants to remove, and throw away, all the pins used in the dress. They would be particularly keen to do so, for if they sleep with one of these pins under their pillow for a week, and then be sure to throw it far away, they too will marry within the year.

Another inanimate object vested with supernatural powers is the kettle. Young girls are warned not to turn a boiling kettle's spout towards the wall, for fear of never finding a husband. This chiding probably resulted from some girl leaving a steam stain on the wall in days gone by; her mother, exasperated perhaps, complained that someone who could not carry out even simple household duties without mishap was not ready for other wifely responsibilities. By the same token, if a girl cannot quickly build up a bright, hot fire, she will make a poor marriage.

Yorkshire folk maintain that if a girl walks over a broomstick she will be pregnant before she marries. In African superstition, striking a man with a broom is a dreadful charm, for it will render him impotent, while if a woman is struck with a broom, she will lose her husband to another.

When using your broom to clean out dusty corners, try not to disturb every cobweb — leave a few for luck. This belief grew from the legend that it was a cobweb that hid the baby Jesus from Herod's soldiers, so tearing one down will bring bad luck. An American superstition is not so positive, saying that cobwebs in the kitchen will encourage the man of the house to stray . . . an indictment with overtones as obvious as those pertaining to kettles.

The Daily Round

You are what you eat — and drink. "Tea for two, and two for tea" runs the old song; this beverage is almost universal and many charms and superstitions surround its preparation and consumption. Reading the future from tea-leaves is quite a science, and an elaborate divination code based on the shapes and figures formed by the leaves left in the cup has afforded people pleasure over time.

One of the most widely accepted omens is that a single leaf floating on the surface of the tea represents a visitor. This stranger will be a man if the stalk is hard, a woman if it is soft. If the enquirer thinks the stranger is a prospective marriage partner, then the number of months before a wedding can be ascertained by placing the piece on the back of the hand and then clapping both hands together in an effort to dislodge it — the number of claps representing the number of months.

Less well-known is the belief that bubbles in the drink indicate kisses for the drinker. Also obscure is the North English assertion that young girls should not allow men to pour their tea for them, or they would be seduced and bring shame to their family — one wonders, perhaps, whether a dippy maiden aunt confused this with 'demon alcohol'. Still, the superstition has flourished and spread with a few variations, for in Wales it is said that if two women pour tea from the same pot, one of them will have a baby within a year.

People have different ways of making a cup of tea, and the various rituals are all fraught with significance. For instance, young girls who put milk into their tea before adding sugar will risk becoming spinsters. If they overcome this hurdle, they should still take care when sitting down to actually drink their tea, particularly if they are imbibing in the presence of a sweetheart. Sitting at the corner of a table results in old maid-hood, as does sitting on the table and, worst of all, swinging the legs. Once again, these superstitions appear to have been conveniently invented by mothers attempting to instil some manners in their offspring.

Clothing needs to be carefully considered also. Robert Herrick was well aware of the effect a certain dress or item of clothing could have upon the sensibilities:

"A sweet disorder in the dress

Kindles in clothes a wantonness
A lawn about the shoulders thrown
into a fine distraction . . .
A careless shoestring in whose tie
I see a wild civility
Does more bewitch me, than when Art
is too precise in every Part."

Starting with the basics, ladies' underwear has been associated with many portents and omens. There is a ribald suggestion that if any item of a girl's underwear falls down for no apparent reason, she is wondering about her lover. Should the same thing happen to a married woman, she should be aware this means she is the subject of gossip — and that people are talking about her having an extra-marital affair, real or imagined. Pantyhose curling up from the bottom indicate a romantic surprise is in the offing. Stockings also augur well for matters of the heart (in addition to being far more downright sexy than pantyhose). If the suspender clasp takes more than three attempts to close, you will meet a handsome stranger that day.

Even petticoats and slips can be used in love divination, as shown in this delightful American verse:

"This Friday night while going to bed
I put my petticoat under my head
To dream of the living and not of the dead
To dream of the man I am to wed.
The colour of his eyes, the colour of his hair
The colour of the clothes he is to wear
And the night the wedding will be."

Superstitions about shoes and boots abound. Of particular interest to the young girl desirous of knowing whether she would wed was this old rhyme about the way she had worn her shoes down:

"Tip at the toe, live to see woe

61

Wear at the side, live to be a bride
Wear at the ball, live to spend all
Wear at the heel, live to save a deal."

Even shoelaces carry omens and portents about the state of
your love life. It is lucky to find a knot in your shoelaces and
you should make a wish as you knot someone else's. Untied
shoelaces, according to the Americans ". . . are a sure sign and
true that, at that very moment, your true love thinks of
you."

Shoes themselves are not a well-omened gift for lovers or
engaged couples to exchange. Perhaps this harks back to the
ancient Jewish custom whereby, if a marriage proposal is
refused, then both parties loosen their shoes.

The Mystic Order of Itches and Scratches

Ordinary bodily functions take on a distinctly extra-ordinary
importance when viewed through a rosy haze of romantic
daydreaming.

An itching or tingling sensation on the lip means someone
is going to kiss you, or wishes they could. An itching elbow
means you will shortly sleep in a strange bed — with, one
assumes, a stranger. An itching nose is said, in some countries,
to be a sign that you have an unknown admirer, although the
Canadians say it could mean one of four things:

"You'll be angry, see a stranger
Kiss a fool, or be in danger."

If any of these itches are the result of a flea bite, the Germans
say this means a kiss is coming, particularly if the bite was on
the hand or neck.

A sudden nose bleed is usually an ill-omen for the person's
health, although if it can be staged in the presence of a desired
one, it is a sign that the affection will be returned. An
accidental sneeze as distinct from one caused by the 'flu', can
mean many things. The ancients thought this little 'explosion'

in the head was a message from the gods, and a popular rhyme goes:

> "Once a wish, twice a kiss,
> three times something better."

People in Cornwall add:

> "Sneeze on a Sunday morning fasting
> Enjoy your true love everlasting."

Specifically, if a young girl sneezes on a Tuesday, it means she will kiss a stranger within the week. Sneezing on a Saturday will have prompter results, enabling her to meet her true love on the morrow. The Chinese are also specific on the best timing for sneezes, claiming that sneezes should be confined within the hours of 1 am and 3 am, thus ensuring that your intended will think of you to the exclusion of all others.

Interestingly, modern science suggests sneezing is not as innocent as it seems, for there may be a connection between the tissues of the nose and the penis. These boffins in their white coats earnestly assure us that a man is most likely to sneeze after sex — so don't worry that your partner may have a cold, for sneezing at that particular moment indicates a full and happy sex life.

The sudden sensation of ringing in the ears, according to a cryptic couplet from Britain, indicates someone is talking about you — with praise, if the ringing is in the right ear, with annoyance if in the left, as follows:

> "Left your mother, Right your lover."

Even winking can be a powerful love charm to control destiny or make a wish come true. In Texas, a girl will wink at the brightest star she can see before going to bed, as a means of guaranteeing her sweetheart's affections. Again the Chinese are a little more precise — an involuntary, not deliberate winking of the left eye will make your lover think of you, although the right eye does not augur well, with any twitching or winking presaging an accident — if this occurs, you are better off staying at home.

Traditional Chinese love lore has a great deal to say about the meanings of freckles or moles on the body. A cautious Chinese mother would counsel her daughter against the advances of a suitor with a mole just in front of his left ear, meaning he had a weakness for the opposite sex, and would not remain faithful to her. Similarly, a wrinkle in the same spot would indicate the man would be a widower — any Chinese parent, knowing this, would not send a daughter 'into the mouth of a tiger' and the chances are he would remain unmarried. The man with a mole right in the middle of his forehead was a far safer option — slow, steady, yet honest and trustworthy.

Perhaps most fortunate of all is the young Chinese girl with a mole on her left breast, for she will grow up to be irresistible and to have the choice of any man she wants. Such superstitions are not confined exclusively to the East; the doughty Queen Victoria is said to have been delighted when a fortune-teller advised her she was due for an early and happy marriage because she had a mole on her left eyebrow.

The Birds and the Bees

Birds, which have the mysterious gift of flight denied to earthbound men, were regarded by our forebears as semi-divine beings, bringing messages from the heavens.

As early as the 12th century B.C., birds were being used by Chinese street fortune-tellers to divine the future according to the I Ching, or Book of Changes. A girl would ask a question regarding her romantic destiny and the bird would indicate, with its beak, one of a number of paper strips carrying a passage from the sacred book, which is then interpreted by the fortune teller.

Long after the coming of Christianity, the art of orni-thomancy or divination by birds, was constantly practised. Certain birds were particularly auspicious regarding matters of the heart. The stork, of course, has long been associated with happy matters of love and fidelity — in European superstition, if two lovers see a pair of storks together, they can expect to conceive a child before very long. Another lanky bird, the crane, mates for life, and the Japanese revere the bird as a symbol of long-lasting love.

Another bird that is the subject of omens and superstitions is the cuckoo. Should a young man remove his shoes at the time he hears the cuckoo's first call, and find a hair inside, it will be the same colour as that of his future wife. The bird's song can also tell an unmarried girl about her future. The number of notes she first hears it sing will indicate the number of years she must wait to wed. Later in the cuckoo-season, she can go to a cherry tree, shake it and say:

> "Cuckoo, cuckoo, cherry-tree
> How many years afore I marry?"

Tradition says that the dove is the one bird into which the Devil cannot turn himself, and consequently it has been regarded as sacred since early times. It is also credited with being the messenger of Venus and as such is a good omen, especially to lovers. According to Indian folklore, the bird actually contains the soul of a lover and great misfortune will follow the killing of one.

On both sides of the Atlantic, crows and magpies have been widely associated with witchcraft and fortune-telling. The number of them seen also indicates the future of the witness, according to the following rhyme:

> "One — sorrow
> two — mirth
> Three a wedding,
> four a birth."

The peacock, perhaps because of its beauty and proud manner, has always played a prominent part in myth and fable. Many people believe it is unlucky to wear the feathers and if they are kept as decorations in the house, a Scottish superstition warns that there will be no weddings in that home.

The swallow, however, is a bird of blessing in most parts of England and Western Europe. Its arrival heralds summertime which, being the season of plenty, is associated with fertility. It is a very good sign for the inhabitants if a swallow nests under the eaves of a house.

Christian tradition revered bees as "the little winged servants of God", admiring their industry and sweet produce. They are said to hate blasphemy and unchastity and will attack a person they suspect of being unfaithful or rude. It used to be thought that if a girl could walk through a swarm of bees without coming to harm, then she was a virgin. A masochistic Frenchman even regards the bee sting as a potent aphrodisiac, and therefore a positive omen of imminent amatory success with a desired lady.

The ladybird was closely associated with the Egyptian goddess, Isis, and also with the Virgin Mary — its name deriving from the original "Our Lady's Bird". In Norfolk it is affectionately known as "Bishy Bishy Barnaby" and a child, on finding one, should set it on the back of his hand, puff gently to make it fly off, and watch where it goes — this being the direction a future lover would travel from:

> "Bless you, bless you burnie bee
> Tell me when my wedding day will be
> If it be tomorrow day
> Take your wings and fly away
> Fly to the East, fly to the West
> Fly to him that I love the best."

GETTING THE TIMING RIGHT

All around the world, the better-known feasts and rituals of Hallowe'en, All Saints Day, Midsummer Solstice, Valentine's Day and many more are celebrated. All have special love rites and charms which work best at that particular time.

For instance, in the northern hemisphere, Carling Sunday (the fifth in Lent) is a most auspicious marriage divination day. The name derives from the custom of eating carlins — or peas fried in butter on this day. A group of young people would gather around a plate of these, and spoon out the peas one at a time — the person to whom the last pea fell, would be the first to marry.

Leap Years are also lucky for lovers, and for girls, in particular — for they can propose to a sweetheart at any time during the year, without fear of rejection. The Scots do, however, add a potentially embarrassing condition: when the girl pops the question, she must wear something red — for being a 'scarlet woman', perhaps?

Lunatics and Starry Eyed Lovers

Many moon superstitions, past and present, show distinct traces of moon worship and of astrological doctrines concerning the influence of heavenly bodies on the lives of men.

> "They dined on mince and slices of quince
> Which they ate with a runcible spoon
> And hand in hand, on the edge of the sand
> They danced by the light of the moon."

So wrote the delightfully dotty Edward Lear. He was probably fortunate not to have been around several hundred years ago, when the moon was officially believed to be a prime cause of madness and a 'lunatic' was someone 'afflicted with a period of fatuity in the period following the full moon'.

Since time immemorial, it has been considered that the moon not only controls the tides — it also controls the moods, fertility and fortunes of women, as Christopher Fry observed:

> ". . . the moon is nothing but a circumabulating aphrodisiac, divinely subsidised to provide the world with a rising birthrate."

For instance, in ancient Mesopotamia Astarte, the goddess of love, was usually depicted wearing a crescent moon headdress which, because of its resemblance to horns, had sexual overtones. Also, in classical tradition, the moon was a sister to a male sun and it became the domain of the Greek goddess Artemis and her Roman counterpart, the huntress Diana. Diana lives on to the present day as the patroness of some latter-day witch covens, a role which her traditional mastery of night-flying makes her well suited to play.

The ancient people of Babylonia and Egypt, along with many primitive tribes, attributed the onset of menstruation to the moon, which was felt to defile young girls. Even today, the Papuan natives of New Guinea say the moon is responsible for the pregnancy itself, as have the Buddhists for many centuries — Buddha himself being moon-begotten. The Maoris go one step further, saying that the moon is the woman's real husband, while the human version is just a temporary substitute. Australian Aborigines also believe their women-folk belong to the moon and Eskimo mothers warn their daughters not to look too long at the moon, lest they become pregnant.

An Indian woman from the American South-West who wishes to become pregnant will stand naked over a bucket of water in which the rays of the moon are reflected. A Central European farmer's wife would drink such water, and then lie naked in a field, exposing her body to the moon when it is in its first and last quarters — that is, when it is 'horned'.

Other superstitions claim that intercourse at the 'dark' of the moon will never lead to a pregnancy and that the sex of the child depends on whether or not the moon had a halo around it at the time of conception.

As the moon waxed and waned, so it affected all other growing and changing things. Certain phases are regarded as auspicious for a life-event — for instance, in the Orkneys, a marriage celebrated under a waning moon will never be fruitful. The time of the full moon is most usually said to be a good time to cure illnesses and for a young person to determine whether they will marry; the ideal time for a boy and girl to meet and fall in love was the seventh day of the full moon. Herefordshire girls looked at the first full moon after New Year through a silk handkerchief and then examined its reflection in a bucket of water. Each reflection indicated a year to wait before marriage.

In America's Tennessee, it is the new moon which is best used as a love omen. A young girl should look at it over her right shoulder, take three steps backwards and say these words in order to ascertain her romantic future:

"New moon, new moon, true and bright
If I am to take a lover, let me dream of him tonight
If I am to marry far, let me hear a bird cry
If I am to marry near, let me hear a cow low
If I am to marry never, let me hear a hammer knock."

In some pagan mythologies, stars and planets were thought to be human souls or great heroes raised after death to dwell in glory in the skies. Astrologers still regard the stars as governing mens' lives and traces of these ancient notions can be seen in many superstitious beliefs. For instance, if any young, unmarried person wishes to find out who their future mate will be, they should count seven stars in the heavens for seven successive nights. The first person they shake hands with on the eighth day will provide a clue as to the identity of the husband or wife.

The following rhyme, recited when the first star of evening is sighted is of course, universal in its appeal:

"Star light, star bright, first star I see tonight
Wish I may, wish I might, have the wish I wish tonight."

After all, who has not fondly whispered this to obtain a romantic objective in their life, remembering always what Pinocchio said in Walt Disney's classic cartoon fantasy — ". . . makes no difference who you are, when you wish upon a star, your dreams come true."

A number of myths and legends have been woven around the sparkling stars. One of the prettiest I know is that of the Chinese Shepherd and the Weaver Girl. These two legendary lovers are destined to meet only once a year on the seventh evening of the seventh moon. The shepherd is the star Aquila and the weaver Girl is Vega — and they are separated by the Milky Way. If it does not rain on this night, magpies build a bridge across the Milky Way with the shadows of their wings so the two may run to each other. Chinese girls will pray for good weather on that night so the bridge is not washed away, believing that the happiness of the Weaver Girl will bring about their own.

Hallowe'en

Long ago, when the new year was said to begin on November 1, Hallowe'en was the original New Year's Eve, and highly thought of as a time for good luck and well-wishing. It has continued to augur well for charms designed to bring about romantic happiness. For instance, to guarantee a dream of her future love on Hallowe'en, a young girl could place her shoes in the form of a "T", a potent talisman representing the hammer of the Scandinavian god, Thor. She then said:

"Hoping this Hallow's Eve my true love to see
I place my shoes in the form of a T."

An unmarried daughter of the house could sleep with a

large apple under her pillow to bring a vision of her true love. A more complicated charm involved her standing before her looking glass while eating the apple and brushing her hair — the face of her future husband would be seen in the reflection, standing beside her.

In the Middle Ages, the hazel was invested with magical powers and forked hazel wands, which had to be cut on St. John's Eve, were used in searches for water and treasure buried underground. The hazel's supernatural prowess came to the fore on Hallowe'en, with the nuts playing a part in several traditional love divination games.

A popular one was for young girls to place a line of hazelnuts on a hot grate, naming each one for a potential suitor, and say:

> "If you love me, pop and fly
> If you hate me, burn and die."

If the nut burst with a loud popping noise, then its namesake was 'hot' with passion for the girl who had made the enquiry. If it smouldered lackadaisically, or did nothing at all, then so, unfortunately, would the lad in question.

Even betrothed couples would use hazelnuts to check on the status of the romance. Both boy and girl would select a nut and place them in the fire. If they jumped together in the heat, all was well, but woe betide the person whose nut leapt out of the fireplace for this meant that they were — or were planning to be — unfaithful.

The luckiest hazelnut for anyone to find on Hallowe'en would have two kernels. If the finder ate one kernel in silence and managed to induce his partner to eat the other, long-lasting love and fidelity in marriage would be assured.

A Hallowe'en charm from Cardiganshire in Wales for ivy leaves is clearly related to this use of nuts in charms and divination. Two ivy leaves would be thrown on the fire — a pointed one for the man and a rounded one for the woman. If the leaves jumped apart, a quarrel was in the offing; if they jumped together, then the couple they represented would marry.

A girl could use ivy to divine her future husband by placing three ivy leaves to her breast and murmuring the spell:

"Ivy, ivy, I love you
in my bosom I put you
The first young man I do see
He shall my husband be."

The leaves could also be used by a young man desirous of knowing what his future wife would be like. A fellow would gather ten leaves on Hallowe'en, put one in his breast pocket and the others under his pillow. He would then dream of her for nine successive nights.

Salt, being incorruptible and therefore a symbol of eternal life and immortality, is included in many charms. A rather more sombre Hallowe'en divination game practised on the Isle of Man was for each person to upturn a thimbleful of salt on their empty plate after eating and leave it till morning. If any of the little mounds had fallen, the person on whose plate it stood would die or travel far away within the coming year. Marriage omens could also be read from whether the salt was moist or dried out.

America remains the bastion of Hallowe'en traditions, and many divination games practised today are hundreds of years old. A love charm from Tennessee for you to try — catch a snail and shut it up in a box or on a covered dish for the night. In the morning, your lover's initials will be traced in a silvery trail on the surface. An even older custom requires the snail to be left to wander over freshly-raked ashes in a hearth — again, leaving a clue as to the future mate's identity in the shape of a letter or number.

If a girl's home is nearby a stream or a pool, she should secretly visit it at midnight on Hallowe'en, for the moonlight will illuminate a reflection of her future husband in the water. Should she be wary of being abroad on this night, she may go during the day, carrying a glass containing a broken egg. When the egg is dropped into the water, it will assume shapes, giving her clues as to the man she will marry and the number of children she will bear.

Christmas and New Year

The festive season is traditionally a time of good will and highly auspicious for omens and signs. The holly and the mistletoe are two plants which are universal in their appeal, being symbols of love and affection at this happy time.

The use of holly as a household decoration has its roots in the Roman festival of Saturnalia, which was celebrated in December. The Romans regarded red as a vital, conquering colour, so the scarlet berries were a good portent. Traditionally, the prickly leaves were thought to be male, and the smooth ones female.

A Scottish divination charm whereby a Highland lassie could induce dreams of a mate required her to go out, in silence, at midnight on Christmas Eve and gather nine she-holly leaves. These had to be tied with nine knots in a handkerchief and laid under the pillow before retiring. The future husband would then appear in a dream, but only if complete silence had been observed. She also had to be most careful that she did not mistakenly pick any male leaves in the dark, for these would bode ill for her ability to conceive.

The pretty, pearly berries of the mistletoe are a happy love charm, bringing prosperity and good fortune to all who embrace beneath a bough. Kissing under the mistletoe appears to be a purely English custom, of which no trace can be found in other countries unless the English have settled there. In fact, the supposedly reserved British were once "much given to kissing" and foreign writers in the 16th and 17th centuries were wont to comment on the frequency with which they kissed perfect strangers, in meeting for the first time.

When standing under the mistletoe, a girl cannot refuse to be kissed by anyone who asks her and young men used to carry branches as trophies, plucking a berry for every kiss they garnished. Interestingly, it is still said in some parts of rural England that a girl should take care that she is kissed under the mistletoe, at least once before her wedding, otherwise she will never bear children.

Perhaps the origins of the mistletoe's kissing status may be found in the England of old — sacred to pre-Christian religions, the Druids referred to mistletoe as "The Golden Bough". They worshipped the berries, believing them to be droplets of seminal fluid of the oak on which it throve. Although the Druids regarded it as a holy fertility charm, ancient Norwegian lore is more pragmatic; their sages claim that a spoiled young prince was punished for a crime by never again being able to kiss a pretty girl, and being forced to look on as others did so.

New Year's Eve, with its atmosphere of fresh beginnings and optimism, augurs well for love divination. With plenty of festive meals being served in the house, an unmarried girl in Scotland would beg the kitchen for a wishbone — or "merrythought" — to be retained, unbroken, for use in her romantic machinations. The easiest method was for two people to clasp either end of the bone and tug — with the larger piece bestowing a wish-come-true on the holder. A more fiddly — and amusing game was for the enquirer to drill a tiny hole in the flat piece at the top of the wishbone and, sitting it on her nose like a pair of spectacles, try to pass a length of red cotton through the hole. As many times as she failed to perform this task, so many years must she wait before she married. Boys and girls would both angle for a second wishbone and wedge it in the lintel over the front door on New Year's Eve. The first person to enter would be their future partner.

Eggs are a traditional ingredient of many aphrodisiacal recipes. Eros, the Greek god of love, was said to have been born of an egg; the yolks are popularly credited with being able to increase sperm; and, the shell also carries ancient symbolism. Both Persian and Egyptian brides would throw an egg against the wall on their wedding night in the hope that their virginity would 'break' as easily. The supreme symbol of fertility and new beginnings, they are at their most magical at the time of the birth of a new year. A Welsh charm requires the yolk of a hard-boiled egg to be removed and the whole packed with salt. Eating this in silence before going to bed will result — along with indigestion, one supposes — in dreams of a future lover. Be very careful to punch a hole in the base of the empty shell when you have finished eating, for otherwise witches will use them as transport out to sea, where they will cause shipwrecks.

Mirrors and candles seem quite ordinary items to have around the house yet they, too, come into their magical own when Christmas and New Year come around. Accidentally snuffing a candle is a sure sign of a wedding, as are three candles burning in a room. A very old English spell to recall an absent lover required a girl to press three pins half-way down a candle, light it in front of a window and say:

"It's not the candle alone I mean to stick
but . . .'s heart I mean to prick
Whether he be asleep or awake
I'll have him come to me and speak."

The wandering one would have arrived by the time the candle burned down to the pins. This spell was also employed by witches when compelling their subjects to submit to their directions.

Similarly, an unfaithful sweetheart could be forced to smartly toe the line by a German girl who lit a candle at both ends and then recited the Paternoster aloud three times. The fellow's passion for the girl would increase three-fold and he would rapidly return to her side.

Mirrors have been used on both sides of the Atlantic to divine the identity of a future lover, in much the same way as seers use a crystal ball. Various methods were used by English girls in the 19th century who wanted to know how many years would pass before they were married. In one, the girl had to stand on a stone with her back to the first full moon after New Year, holding a mirror in her hand. She would see the moon and stars' reflections — the number of illuminations counted represented the number of years before her wedding. In the American Deep South, if a young belle holds a mirror over a pool of water she will see on it the image of her intended. Similarly, by sleeping with a mirror under her pillow on New Year's Eve, a Scottish lass will dream of her future husband.

Not all New Year celebrations are exclusive to December 31st throughout the world. Chinese New Year is held early in the year, the actual date being adjusted to when the most auspicious omens are evident. Chinese girls may take advantage of the potent atmosphere to petition the goddess Kuan-Yin. As the goddess of mercy, she is often pictured with a child in her arms, symbolising hope for the lonely and childless, and would provide help in matters of the heart. The usual method was for the enquirer to write her name, a religious text and her particular request on a piece of parchment, named a 'fu'. This was then burned at an altar, and the smoke carried the message to the gods in the clouds.

The Chinese believe that everything in life is pre-destined. With this in mind, it is only natural that two persons born under the influence of opposing New Year animals should not marry. Even today, many Malay Chinese parents like to know the animal controlling the destiny of their child's proposed marriage partner, to see whether it is in harmony with that of their own child.

St. Agnes' Eve

St. Agnes' Eve (January 20) was also a significant night for dreams and visions in the northern hemisphere. St. Agnes is the patron saint of virgins — she herself refused to marry a man not of her choice and was put to death for her refusal. In days past girls would, on this night, make a 'Dumb Cake' of eggs, water, flour and salt, prepared in silence and fasting. Each girl would then mark her initials on the cake, and recite the following:

> "Sweet St. Agnes, work thy fast
> If ever I be to marry man,
> or ever man to marry me
> I hope him this night to see."

The cake was then set amongst the coals, not the oven, so as to bake slowly throughout the night. At midnight, the wraith of her future mate would turn it for her and prick his initials next to hers on the cake with a fork.

In some parts of northern England, two or more girls would meet to make the cake; they would then divide it equally and walk backwards to their rooms, where they would eat their portions in silence before sleeping, then dreaming of their future husbands.

Bachelors would also try to induce an apparition of their wife to be on St. Agnes' Eve or New Year's Eve, by eating a raw red herring — bones and all — before retiring.

Valentine's Day

When Christianity became the official religion of the Roman Empire by edict of the Emperor Constantine, religious leaders immediately started to do away with pagan festivals. One of the most effective methods was the substitution of a Christian observance for a pagan one. Hence, the martyrdom of St. Valentine, a man renowned for his chastity, who was stoned to death in 269 A.D., has been celebrated on this day ever since — even though his character appears unconnected with the day's traditional customs. It was, in fact, originally known as "Lupercalia", being the Roman festival of youth. It was sacred to the Queen of Heaven and protector of women, Juno, wife of Jupiter, who was said to bestow her blessing on courtship rituals or marriages celebrated that day and to give girls good luck when playing romantic games of chance. For instance, sweethearts for the day were often drawn by lottery. Girls and boys would have frantically hoped for the best as they plunged their hands into a barrel of named slips of paper as the watching crowd sang:

> "Thou art my love and I art thine
> I draw . . . for my Valentine."

The girl had to call out the name on the piece of paper at the appropriate spot, and he would come forward from the crowd to claim her.

A less publicly embarrassing game for a Roman girl on Lupercalia was to write the name of her favourites on small pieces of paper, roll them in moist clay and drop them in water. The slip that first floated to the surface would bear the name of the future sweetheart. A variation of this game, interestingly, was still being played in 18th century England, and a very lucky gift was a small hollow, waterproof locket containing a lover's name. These were often prettily coloured and blind-folded girls had to fish them out of a bowl of water, in much the same way as bobbing for apples.

The power of a chance occurrence to change your life — at least for a day — still appears in the tradition that the first member of the opposite sex seen on Valentine's Day will be the future partner. (By the way, the Welsh say your chances of ensuring this really is your Valentine are increased if you wear a large yellow crocus in your buttonhole, this being the special flower for the day.)

Birds are usually mating in both Britain and America by mid-February. Since all nature seemed to be preoccupied with the beginning of a new cycle of pairing off males and females, it was only natural that humans should do the same thing. This gave rise to many superstitions regarding the first bird seen on St. Valentine's Day by a girl, for it was said to indicate what sort of man her husband would be. For instance, a blackbird meant a clergyman or priest; a goldfinch (or any yellow bird for that matter) a rich man; a crossbill was an argumentative, mean man; and doves and bluebirds were good and happy men respectively. However, should she see or hear a woodpecker on Valentine's Day she would never marry.

Traditional verses were laboriously copied onto parchment and despatched by special bearer to the loved one on Valentine's Day. For instance:

"Good morning to you, Valentine
Curl your locks as I do mine

78

One before and two behind
Good morning to you, Valentine."

The sender would later call on the subject of his desire and
hope to see her ringlets thus arranged, to indicate she
returned his affection.

Such tokens and gestures were all-important in many
cultures leading up to this present century. Quite simply,
would-be lovers had very little — if any — opportunity to be
alone together without a chaperone. Even if they had been
able to meet and declare their feelings, the tyranny of distance,
in pre-motor car and telephone days, dictated they rely on
gifts and letters. Valentines were honour-bound to offer each
other a lover's gift on this day; a card accompanying a
traditional gift of scented and embroidered kid gloves might
read:

"The rose is red, the violets blue
Gillies are sweet and so are you
These are the words you bid me say
For a pair of new gloves on Valentine's Day."

These rhymes and verses eventually burgeoned into the
Valentine's Day greeting card industry we have today. Samuel
Pepys, author of the famous diaries, says the first Valentine,
appropriately illustrated with a rose, appeared on February
14, 1667. Before the end of the 17th century, printers began
producing limited numbers of cards with verses and sketches.
Postal rates were so high that most of these Valentines were
delivered by hand. Incidentally, never sign a Valentine's card,
for it is very unlucky to do so.

Not all people will receive a card or a kiss on Valentine's
Day. This has been, traditionally, a far more devastating state
of affairs for a girl than a boy. Be grateful we no longer have
customs such as "pease-dusting" in the world. In days gone
by, a lass who had not been courted on Valentine's Day would
be set upon by the other young folk in the village and rubbed
all over with pease-straw, just to add to her humiliation. No

wonder the fate of being an 'old maid' was so abhorred though, to be fair, the same derisory consolation was given by village girls to a youth who had lost his sweetheart to another during the Valentine's Day festivities.

A friend who was more gentle in her ministrations might suggest the bereft girl try this peas-y charm to get her love life back on track. When shelling a basketful of peas, she should look for a pod containing nine perfect peas (which is quite an easy task). She then had to place the pod over the front door — the first young man who walked under it would be seized by the urge to marry her. Similarly if, when laying the pod on the lintel, she murmurs the name of another woman in the house, the next male visitor would be that woman's Valentine.

Midsummer Madness

"Roll out those lazy, hazy, crazy days of summer!" goes the popular song, as people, clothing and — occasionally — morals relax and loosen in the heat.

Not only does the warmth have a soporific effect; in the northern hemisphere May Day and Midsummer Solstice are times of great magical significance. May Day was originally Beltane, the Celtic festival of sun-worship, and huge bonfires were lit all over the countryside to mark the occasion. Rituals are employed by would-be lovers on this day which are linked to this heritage. For instance, in France, near Valenciennes, young men would hang branches of horse beech outside their sweethearts' doors as a symbol of their devotion. It was particularly appropriate for this task, as it is an evergreen, will grow in any sort of soil and produces nuts at a prolific rate.

Many other plants were believed to convey the fertilising powers of nature into the community, notably the may and the hawthorn:

> "There's not a budding girl or boy this day
> But has got up and gone to bring in May'

wrote Robert Herrick, referring to the custom of Englishmen to stick branches of birch into the ground outside their lady's house and hand a garland of may flowers over her lintel, thus inviting her to "go a-maying", a lusty euphemism for love-making. The girl, however, could have been wary of the pretty pink and white blossom — it is, after all, a fairy flower and unsafe for humans to wear or touch. Witness this Somerset poem referring to "The Love Talker", a fairy who would wander the forests in the likeness of a handsome man, seducing the countryside's maidens:

> "O my love wore a garland of May
> and she looked so nice and neat;
> to her pretty little feet,
> till she met her false lover in the dew."

Young girls who met this man found him irresistible; however, he vanished after making love to them and they never saw him again.

The hawthorn tree was said to contain the spirit of the woodfolk and to symbolise fertility and harvest. It was also a trysting-place for sweethearts, according to Goldsmith:

> "The hawthorn bush with seats beneath the shade
> For talking age and whispering lovers was made."

May Day rites, which have their origin in pagan fertility rituals, included the crowning of a May Queen, Morris dancing, traditional plays, bawdy singing and dancing around the maypole. Hawthorn wood was frequently used to make the maypole and the hobby-horses which featured in traditional merry-making.

The flowering branches could be used in marriage divination games. One required a girl to go out early on May Day morn to gather the red and white flowers, taking care not to speak to anyone, for if she did she would not marry in the coming year. She then fashioned them into a hoop which was hung on the sign-post at four lane-ends on May Day eve. In the morning, she would run to see which way the wind had blown it in the night, for her husband would come from that direction. If it had blown away altogether, she would not marry at all.

"Watching in the church porch", usually performed on Midsummer's Eve, was a form of marriage divination that was well-known in most parts of Europe until the latter half of the 19th century. The enquirer went to the church porch at 11 o'clock and laid a bunch of may flowers on the church stoop. He or she then went away, returning at midnight, just before the clock struck. If a bridal procession was seen passing into the church, marriage was foretold within the year and the number of bridesmaids denoted how many months would elapse before the wedding. If nothing happened, it meant that the watcher would not marry that year, though a coffin carried by ghostly bearers denoted they would die unwed.

Sage leaves have been used for marriage divination and in remedies for various ills. A charm to help a young person to see his or her marriage partner, either in bodily form or as a vision, entailed the charmer to pick twelve sage leaves at midnight, one for each time the clock struck. The future wife or husband would then be seen, appearing over the enquirer's left shoulder.

Another Midsummer's Eve charm for a girl seeking news of her lover was to go into the garden, pluck a handful of sage leaves and scatter them to the winds. As she did so, a vision of where her sweetheart was and what he was doing would appear. If she was frightened by what she saw, she could run to a nearby beech tree for sanctuary, and pray to the gods for their favour — because it was a holy tree, and sacred to the Druids, requests would go heavenwards with haste.

Many legends are told of rosemary, which is both a holy and magical plant in popular tradition. It has long signified remembrance and is used in Anzac Day wreaths when returned servicemen pay tribute to their comrades. Rosemary was used in charms to secure success in enterprises or to renew youth, and also in love charms and marriage spells. A simple charm suggests rosemary be put in a pillow slip, along with a piece of silver, to encourage dreams of a future mate. Another recommends that a saucer of flour be placed under a rosemary bush on Midsummer Eve — in the morning a clue could be drawn from the flour's appearance as to the husband's nature and name.

The sweet smell of a rose, flowering at the height of summer, has assured this flower of a place in Midsummer love divination. Girls slept with rose and bay leaves under their pillow and pressed them against their heaving maidenly bosoms. Pretty charms entailed gathering and drying roses, whilst reciting the betrothal service from the Book of Common Prayer, and then secreting the powdered petals in the loved one's clothing for the desired effect. Rather more effort was required to recall a straying sweetheart — three roses had to be picked, one buried beneath a yew tree, another laid in a new grave, and the last placed tenderly under the girl's pillow. The fellow had little choice in the matter — he would return to her in three night's time with 'trebled' passion — or he would die.

Similarly, rose-petals scattered over a tomb-stone on Midsummer's Eve would bring a vision of a maiden's future husband, while a posy of roses sprinkled with pigeon's blood, or that of the enquirer, kept under her pillow would reveal his identity in a dream.

If she was not happy with the outcome of any of these charms, she might wait till the following evening. Kissing a red rose, and tucking it into her waistband, she would tiptoe to the henhouse at midnight and tap the rose on the door. If the hen cackled, she would never marry, but if the cock crowed, she would marry before the end of the year.

Like parsley and rosemary, myrtle is said to grow best if it is planted by a woman. Cornish women were advised to spread their petticoats over myrtle when planting it, otherwise it would not flourish. At one time, the flowers were much favoured at weddings; young girls would drink a special infusion of the leaves and flowers on Midsummer's Eve to increase their beauty; and a similar infusion, given by a lover to his dear one, was a sure way of gaining or retaining that person's love. However, in Germany, if a girl is engaged to be married, she should not pick myrtle, as this will cause her wedding to be called off. If it is grown indoors, it will bring good luck to the household and, according to Welsh tradition, a bush set on either side of the front door secured happiness and harmony for those who lived within. Myrtle could be used in a very simple love charm — a girl had only to place a sprig in her Bible, to mark the place where the wedding service began, and sleep with it under her pillow. If she was to marry the man she dreamed of, the myrtle would have disappeared by daybreak. If it remained in the book, he would not marry her.

The pansy was known by country folk as a fertility charm, the two main petals representing a man and a woman, the two smaller ones their children. It is also said to be the magic ingredient used by Puck to seduce Titania in "A Midsummer Night's Dream":

> ". . . and maidens call it love-in-idleness
> Fetch me that herb, the herb I shewed thee once
> The juice of it on sleeping eyelids laid
> will make man or woman madly dote
> upon the next live creature it sees."

Similarly, cinquefoil is a potent summertime fertility charm for women, the symbolic meaning of the plant coming from its ability to draw its leaves together like an affectionate mother protecting her child.

A country name for the orpine plant, often mentioned in medieval Herbals, was "Midsummer Men", because it was once much used in love divination on Midsummer Eve. An enquiring girl would bring in a stalk or cutting and fix it in clay in a convenient crack in the door. If, next morning, the stalk leaned to the right, she knew her lover was true; if to the left, he was false. She could also bring two pieces inside naming one for the man and one for the woman in question. If they were found inclining towards each other after the night had passed, the love-affair would prosper; but if they had swung away from each other during the night, there would be no marriage.

The dainty honeysuckle, as well as being a potent fairy flower, was one of the few which could be used by young men in a love charm, for the warm scent was said to encourage girls to have erotic dreams. He would repeat his name three times over a posy of honeysuckle and then creep into her room and place it on the dressing table while she slept.

HAPPILY EVER AFTER

Marriage was always seen as the desired outcome of any amatory machinations. Whilst living together is today a very acceptable option, it was certainly not always so. Witness the Biblical outpourings of wrath and brimstone in Corinthians: "It is better to marry than burn."

Many societies used to consider that a man and woman who lived together without being married brought ill-fortune to the whole community, for they were in league with the Devil. It was not uncommon for effigies of the offending pair to be burnt, or for their fellow-villagers to drive them out of town to the accompaniment of 'Rough Music' — the latter being much banging of drums, shouting and horn-blowing believed to drive away evil spirits.

Judging by sayings which have come down through the ages, such as 'wedlock's a padlock', the traditional view of marriage is a gloomy one. However, for many people, weddings are a magical time and even the least superstitious will watch for portents of happiness. There is hardly a country in the world where traditions of some kind are not carefully observed so the wedding will go off happily. As a result, the wedding preparations, ceremony and feast have all become loaded with ritual practices to ward off evil and bless the marriage with good fortune and fertility.

What's In a Name?

The first piece of advice offered by superstition to those intending to marry concerns their name, as evidenced by this old English couplet:

"Change the name and not the letter
Change for the worse, and not for the better."

This is now little more than a remembered saying amongst brides, although the superstition which it enshrines is extremely ancient and probably derived from ancient rulings regarding the intermarriage of clans. These taboos against marrying someone from your own family arose amongst primitive man for two reasons. Firstly, he saw that introducing 'fresh blood' improved strength and stamina, much as happened with his herds, and, secondly, it was a mark of bravery to seek a bride from outside the safety of the tribe. (For that same reason, double weddings enjoy chequered popularity — German superstition is adamant that sisters and brothers should not intermarry saying one couple will have an unhappy marriage, as there is not enough luck to go around.)

A more active superstition says that all young women should avoid using their married name — not even write it down for the pleasure of seeing what it looks like — before they are actually wed, or it will never come to be. At one time, this idea extended even to the marking of clothes and house linen in advance; they had to be either left unmarked until after the ceremony or marked with the girls' maiden name. If, immediately after the wedding, someone calls the bride by her old name, purposely or inadvertently, the omen is very bad.

In some parts of England, a woman whose married and maiden names are the same, though she has not married a relation, is believed to have healing powers. Elsewhere, diseases were curable by women who had been twice married to men whose names were the same, though they were unrelated to each other.

The Charmed Circle

"With this ring I thee wed
with my body I thee worship

and with all my worldly goods I thee endow."

Book of Common Prayer: 1662

The ring has no beginning and no end, thus symbolising perfect unity for lovers.

In ancient times, a ring was used as a seal by which orders were signed — therefore, a man giving a ring to his wife showed he was endowing her, as his representative, with all the power he possessed. Interestingly, the word "wed" is Anglo-Saxon, and means "pledge", so the ring is evidence of the pledge given by the groom that he will honour his contract.

At one time, the wearing of rings had more significance than it does now: if a lady or gentleman was willing to marry, they wore a ring on the index finger of the left hand. If they were engaged, they wore it on the second finger; if married, on the third finger; but, if either had no desire to marry, the ring was placed on the little finger.

The third finger on a woman's left hand has always been reserved for an engagement or wedding ring — any other is considered unlucky. This tradition arose from the erroneous belief that an artery or nerve runs directly from this finger to the heart. This finger is also believed to be lucky and to have healing powers when applying any medication; similarly, a white spot on this nail means wealth, or a new lover.

The unbroken circle of the engagement or wedding ring has influenced spells, legends, superstitions and rituals since the days of the Pharoahs. Most women still believe that to wear a wedding ring before marriage brings such bad luck that they will never be married themselves. A wedding ring should not be removed or lent to anyone because if it should be lost the marriage will suffer a similar fate.

A wedding ring should also be new — "A twice-used ring is a fatal ring", although borrowing a wedding ring from a happy bride was, however, considered quite a lucky thing to do. When times are hard, it is not uncommon for an impecunious couple to be unable to afford a wedding ring. The ringed top of the church door key was often used for weddings during the Depression, and in Ireland the parish priest keeps one in readiness to be hired out for a small fee.

> "One ring to rule them all
> One ring to find them
> One ring to bind them all
> and in the darkness find them."
>
> The Lord of the Rings Pt I
> The Fellowship of the Ring
> J.R.R. Tolkien

Wedding rings are usually made of gold, which has supposed magical and curative powers. Even today, wedding rings are rubbed on warts and styes to charm them away. They can also be used in divination by those brave enough to take them off — although in some countries, it is perfectly safe to take or cut off a wedding ring after the birth of the first child. For instance, a ring suspended by a hair will immediately start to spin; if it rotates quickly, then you will only marry once. The same method can be used to divine whether an unborn child is a boy or a girl.

The loss of a wedding ring can augur ill for a marriage — a couple will suffer bad luck if the wife loses her ring later in life. If this happens, her husband should immediately buy another one and place it on her finger, repeating the words of the marriage service as he does so. Dropping the ring before or during the marriage ceremony is also unlucky, particularly if it rolls sharply away from the altar steps. If it came to rest on a gravestone in the floor, it foretold an early death for one of the pair — the groom if it was a man's grave, the bride if it was a woman's.

Engagement rings are not so sacred and therefore possess less magic than wedding rings. Long ago, these betrothal rings were made of gold or silver and fashioned in the shape of a true lover's knot. This consisted of two hoops which could not be separated, one part being given to the man at the betrothal ceremony and the other to the woman. On the marriage day, they were united to form the complete wedding ring.

> "Kissing your hand may make you feel very good, but a
> diamond and safire (sic.) . . . lasts for ever."
>
> Anita Loos: "Gentlemen Prefer Blondes"

Most engagement rings today, however, contain gems. The modern preference is for diamonds, sapphires or rubies, all of which besides being beautiful and valuable, have fortunate properties of one kind or another. The birthstone associated with the wearer's sign of the Zodiac is traditionally said to bring luck to a marriage.

Some gems are associated with bad luck. Pearls are still often disliked, in spite of their beauty, as they signify tears and are therefore not good omens for a happy marriage. Opals are almost universally thought to be unlucky, unless worn by those born in October, because they are changeable and inconsistent. In the East, however, the Chinese believe opals to be particularly fortuitous.

Others are very lucky choices — garnets symbolised constancy, amethyst (so popular as meditative crystals) denoted sincerity and clarity and the sardonyx ensured marital happiness. Carnelians protected the wearer from harm or pain; rubies signified contentment and courage in adversity; the topaz signified fidelity and the sapphire, beloved magic stone of Jupiter, would ward off misery. At one time, the turquoise was a favourite stone, thought to prevent dissension between man and wife. On a more pragmatic note, it also augured well for prosperity and marital finances. Yet, it is the diamond which continues to be the most popular of all gems and symbolises conjugal affection, with sparkling colours that flash from its surface representing future glories and delights for the wearer in life.

"I Plight Thee My Troth"

The day on which a couple buy their engagement ring holds important omens. Wednesday and Saturday augur well for those wanting a peaceful and contented life together. A Friday purchase means the eventual marriage will not be easy and much hard work and heartache will be involved, while a Monday will result in a busy and unpredictable life together.

As with wedding rings, it is very unlucky to lose or break an engagement ring. As the betrothal was sealed by the giving of the ring, so the loss of the latter foretells an ending either because of quarrels between the pair, the death or desertion of one of them or some other unfortunate happening.

A British superstition says that it is unlucky for an engaged couple to hear their banns read in church together; to do so was to risk the dumbness or idiocy of their children. Nor should they accept an invitation to be godparents to the same child, as something will happen to prevent their marriage. This superstition may have its dim origins in the Christian belief that godparents have to be pure, unsullied by earthly lust, in order to guide a child on its spiritual way.

A pretty rural custom suggests that after two people have got engaged, they should take a piece of laurel, break it in half and retain a piece each — as long as they keep them, so their love will flourish. However, should one person not wish to continue the engagement, he or she should present a knife to the other to 'cut' the bonds between them. They were really courting disaster to do so, though — at the very least they risked being subject to a fine for rejecting the other partner.

The Big Day

"Something special. A day amongst days — a red lettuce day."

John Lennon
"Nicely, nicely, Clive"

The choice of month, day and date is very important. Old British almanacs drew upon local superstitions to determine auspicious times at which to wed:

"Married in January's hoar and rime,
Widowed you'll be before your prime.
Married in February's sleepy weather,
Life you'll tread in time together.
Married when March winds shrill and roar
Your home will be on a distant shore.
Married beneath April's changing skies,
A chequered path before you lies.
Married when bees over May blossoms flit,
Strangers around your table will sit.
Married in the month of roses — June,
Life will be one long honeymoon.
Married in July with flowers ablaze,
Bittersweet memories on after days.
Married in August's heat and drowse,
Lover and friend your chosen spouse.
Married in September's golden glow,
Smooth and serene your life will go.
Married when leaves in October are thin
Toil and hardship for your gain.
Married in veils of November mist,
Fortune your wedding ring has kissed.
Married in days on December cheer,
Love's star shines brighter from year to year."

Apart from the fact that the weather in the Northern hemisphere is usually very good in June, this month was also sacred to Jupiter's dear wife, Juno, who bestows special blessings upon women who wed in her month.

May is ill-omened for lovers, being named for Maia, the wife of Vulcan, who was associated with old age and death. In ancient Rome, the month was reserved for making offerings and sacrifices to the newly dead. More recently, when Mary Queen of Scots married James Hepburn, the Earl of Bothwell on May 15, 1567, it boded ill for her, or so said the people who made up this verse at the time:

"The people say
that only wantons marry

in the month of May."

Even today, dour Scottish elders will mutter "Marry in May, live to rue, aye" on hearing of a May wedding; similarly, Christians believe that Lent is an unlucky period for a marriage — "Marry in Lent, live to repent". In fact, during past centuries, religious leaders wielded considerable power: in the 17th century, canons of the Church of England issued the following edict, banning certain times of the year for marriage:

> "When Advent comes, do thou refraine,
> Till Hillary set thee free againe;
> Next Septuagesima saith thee nay,
> But when Lowe Sunday comes, thou may;
> But at Rogation, thou must tarry,
> Till Trinitie shall bid thee marry."

Astrologers contradict the traditional almanac, citing the fruitful sign of Scorpio as a good time to marry throughout the world. As the Scorpion rules the loins, the seat of fertility, many farmers choose Scorpio for moon-planting, and — for obvious reasons — Ozark mountain men claim Scorpio-planted seeds result in large, plump cucumbers!

A Chinese family hoping for a happy marriage for their daughter would endeavour to stage her wedding during the year of the Rat. A certain amount of confusion exists in the Chinese zodiac between the rat and the squirrel, and it is represented by the character 'tzu', which also means 'many sons'. Therefore, a wedding celebrated under the auspices of this year Animal will be blessed with an abundance of male offspring. Interestingly, both East and West pay particular attention to the state of the tides at the time of marriage — a wedding celebrated at ebb tide will not be fruitful, as births are considered most likely to occur at the flowing tide.

Magic Daze

Superstition has a great deal to say about the best days of the week on which to marry, although there are many contradictions from one culture to another. For instance, Friday is traditionally an ill-fated day, generally believed to have earned its unhappy reputation because it was on this day that Adam was tempted by Eve; it was also the day of the crucifixion of Jesus. The Scots, however, consider it a lucky day for courting couples, as do the Norwegians, who hold Friday sacred to Freya, the goddess of love.

Saturday, though by far the most popular day for most couples, is unlucky and said to result in the early death of one of the partners. Traditional German brides would avoid the Australian pay-day, Thursday, believing their marriage would be doomed on this most unlucky day of the whole week. To keep the gods happy, choose a Monday, Tuesday, Wednesday or Sunday for your wedding.

Although it is lucky to choose your birthstone as the gem in your engagement ring, it is unwise to marry on your birthday. By the same token, it is lucky if you and your partner share a birthday, but again, it is not a fortuitous date on which to wed.

As the thirteenth of the month is an inauspicious date on which to commence any new enterprise, few brides would choose to marry on this day without very good reason. Yorkshire girls will avoid December 21 for their weddings, although their neighbours in Lincolnshire considered this to be a very lucky day. Welsh girls can really do no better than to wed on St. Bride's Day, February 1. There is also a charm which may be employed by a new bride wishing to retain the youthful complexion of her wedding day — each year, she should rise early on St. Bride's Day, and rub her face gently with dew.

On the actual wedding day, the bride may anxiously scan the sky for weather omens. In many countries, the superstition exists that if 'the sun hid its face', then disaster and misfortune were on their way.

Evening weddings are not universally popular for this same reason. Melodramatic Italians go further, saying that a wedding conducted after sunset is irrevocably doomed, for not only will the people be unlucky, but they will lose their children and both go to an early grave.

Americans worry if it rains, seeing the drops as evidence that the bride will cry through her married life. Happiest is the bride that the sun shines on, for it signifies heaven tossing warm goodwill and many blessings her way. This adage may well hark back to the times when the wedding ceremony took place at the church door, rather than inside. Undoubtedly, rain would have made this rather miserable.

What Shall I Wear?

"Mind my duvetyne dress above all!
It's golded silvy, the newest sextones with princess effect.
For . . . blue's got out of passion."

James Joyce
"The Ballad of Persse O'Reilly"
Finnegan's Wake

Whatever the prevailing fashion, every bride regards her wedding dress as the most hallowed garment she will ever possess, and any girl given a dress worn by her mother is said to be very lucky indeed.

The colour of the dress is also very important:

> "Blue for a bride and she will rue,
> But dressed in white, her lover's true.
> Yellow's by the saints forsworn,
> And purple makes a bride die aye morn.
> Nothing green for a fine day,
> But pink for the darling buds of May."

Tradition decrees that the bride should be dressed in white, the symbol of innocence and purity. Silver and gold are also lucky and their poor relations, grey and fawn, were formerly chosen by simple brides who preferred a gown that could be worn on other formal occasions.

In China, red is very lucky, signifying prosperity, health and happiness. In Germany, too, attendants will take care to fasten the bride's veil with a thin red ribbon to protect her against evil spirits in her new life. Elsewhere, however, it is an unlucky colour and a Polish bride would have been terrified at the sight of even a tiny drop of blood on her gown, as this was an omen she would not live long. Green was considered, in England, to be a fairy colour and unlucky as the wearer was likely to fall into the hands of the little people. However, the old ballad 'Greensleeves' did make 'kirtles of green' very fashionable amongst court ladies and, in medieval France, it was the colour of true love and worn by couples who were eloping.

Silk is the most widely accepted material for the wedding dress, while satin is said to be unlucky and velvet to presage poverty. There should be no ill-omened designs on the fabric — a Yorkshire girl would be wary of material patterned with birds or vines, as these signify death in that county.

In a traditional Chinese wedding gown, however, bird emblems are likely to figure strongly. Pairs of birds, such as mandarin ducks, orioles, geese and parrots all symbolised constancy and mortal affection. A group of five bats might be embroidered on the bride's bodice, signifying the Five Blessings — old age, wealth, love, virtue and a natural death. Plants such as prunus, cypress and peony would be included in the fabric design, to indicate honour, wealth and longevity. Most spectacularly, the bride and groom would wear rich capes, emblazoned with an embroidered phoenix and dragon, respectively. From early times, the dragon and the phoenix were the special emblems for the emperor and his consort — as 'Emperor and Empress for the day', the pair would enjoy this spectacular garb. The phoenix would also figure in wedding gifts to the bride.

The 'true lovers knot' is a favourite motif for wedding cakes and dresses around the world. These colourful bunches of ribbons, representing the bonds of marriage, and the ties of love and affection, have been part of weddings since the days of old Babylon, when a thread would be taken from each of the bridal couple's gowns and symbolically tied together as part of the wedding ceremony. In the 17th century, brides wore these knots lightly stitched to their dresses, so that young men at the wedding could snatch them as 'bride favours'. Wedding guests would knot ribbons around the bride's flowers or chair, so as to firmly 'tie' her to a future of love and happiness with their good wishes.

Grooms also adopted the symbol of the knot in their own wedding garments — the flower buttonholes are a relic of true lovers' knots and, in many European countries, a man will go to the altar with one of his shoes unknotted, lest witches deprive him of the power on his wedding night of 'untying' his bride's virginity.

The choice and making of The Dress is surrounded by traditional rules the world over. The most common belief is that, as she is commencing a new life, every item she wears or uses should be new, right down to the needle and pins used to sew the dress. The exception to this is the custom of wearing:

> "Something old, something new
> Something borrowed, something blue."

"Old" maintains her link with the past, and is most often a pair of shoes or a piece of heirloom jewellery, while "new" symbolises the future. "Borrowed" — or, in some countries, "stolen" — gives her a link with the present and "blue", preferably sky-blue as the colour of Heaven, symbolises her purity.

Despite the undoubted popularity of pretty underwear as part of bridal trousseaux, the old English custom of 'smock' weddings — whereby a woman went to the altar wearing only her shimmy signifying that her husband was not liable for her debts — gave rise to a bawdy saying that 'a girl who gets married wearing no underwear will be lucky all her life."

The bride's veil is of great importance. An old veil is thought luckier than a new one, particularly if it is borrowed from a woman who is known to be happily married, as the good fortune and fertility of the earlier marriage passes with the veil to the new wearer.

The veil once had the desirable double function of protecting the bride from the evil eye, and keeping her in seclusion, lest the special psychic powers she had at that time bewitch other people. Tradition states that when the groom lifts the veil to kiss the bride, she should cry, or else her married life will be full of tears. This belief stemmed from the English methods of testing for witchcraft: witches were said to be unable to shed more than three tears, and those from the left eye only. Unless the new bride wept profusely from both eyes, it was a sign to the guileless congregation that she had plighted her troth with Satan, instead.

The veil played an important part in a very old English divination game, practised by seamstresses. A long, fair hair from the head of one of the girls was woven through the veil they were busily embroidering. If it broke at the beginning, the wife would die early; if at the end, the husband. If it went right through without breaking, it signified a long and happy life for them both.

Even a modern bride will observe the taboos about wearing her dress before the ceremony. The groom must not see her in it until she enters the church. Nor must she wear the complete outfit before the wedding day, or look at herself in a mirror while wearing it. Certainly the veil should not be tried on at the same time as the dress; many brides put it on for the first time as they leave for church. Some brides even believe that the sewing of the dress should not be completed until the day itself, and leave a few stitches to be completed on the wedding morning.

> "Garter: an elastic ban intended to keep a woman from coming out of her stockings and desolating the country."
> Ambrose Bierce
> "The Devil's Dictionary"

Brides often wear garters, believing them to bring good luck, and for years a garter warm from the leg of a new bride has been considered a cure for most things from impotence to a sore throat.

In 19th century England, the bride's male attendants would pull off her garters before her maids led her to the bedroom; they would then wear them in their hats for luck. The modesty of Victorian times saw this raucous custom tamed somewhat — to make removal more decorous, long white ribbons were attached to the garters and threaded up the bride's leg under her voluminous skirt. Both men and women could compete for the garters — a new bride's garter tucked under a pillow is said to make an unmarried girl dream of her husband-to-be.

Probably due to its association with the Infant Jesus' manger, straw has been used as a fertility charm by young girls of many cultures. A young Yorkshire bride-to-be could make sure of the children she desired in days past by going secretly to the harvest fields on a Friday night before her marriage. For every hoped-for son, she picked a wheat straw; for every daughter, an oat-straw. She then plaited them into a garter which she wore through her wedding and wedding-night. If the garter stayed in place, the omen was good — although, as with so many charms initiated by censorious village elders as a result of social mores — it was said that the method could only be safely used by a virgin. If the lass had lapsed from virtue prior to her wedding, the charm would only bring ill-fortune.

Instead of a garter, a Fijian bride would use a special bangle of shells around her thigh, while a Malay Chinese bride may wear a small silver chain and padlock around her ankle, which is believed to 'lock' her securely out of reach of all devils from the Otherworld. Good luck may also be ensured by wearing an old coin with a hole in the centre, suspended on a red cord, around the neck. Red is an important colour, for it wards off evil.

The Bridal Bouquet

Various plants and flowers are believed to be lucky for a bride to carry or wear on her dress or in her hair. Most people would be familiar with a bride holding a bouquet of roses — this custom harks back to Roman times, when roses were used to deck statues of the god Hymen by newly-weds seeking blessings on their marriage. However, the same wedding guests might look askance at a bride wearing a wreath of oregano, although this was most popular amongst young Greek girls in classical times, being a symbol of fertility and birth:

"And the sweet marjoram with your garden paint
On Simor's shores fair Venus raised the plant
Which from the Goddess's touch, derived her scent."

Rene Rapin

Blue crocus were fashioned into wreaths for both the bride and groom to wear, as were bluebells in later Roman times. Hazel wands were woven into caps for brides to wear, with flowers or jewels poked through the criss-crossed bands. This was the origin of the 20th century 'Juliet' cap, so winsome when worn by curly-headed girls, who pull ringlets through the gaps in the mesh.

Wallflowers were especial favourites of Scottish brides, owing to the romantic story surrounding their beginnings. Apparently, the beautiful Elizabeth, daughter of the doughty Earl of March, fell in love with a handsome soldier, but her father forbade her to meet with him. Heartbroken, she attempted to climb down the wall of her prison tower to her lover's waiting arms, only to fall and kill herself. From the spot where she fell grew a wallflower, which twined around the tower, and her lover plucked one and carried it with him for the rest of his life in her memory. So — it is not surprising that a Scottish bride will ask for wallflowers to be twisted around the pews in the church, or give them to her maids to include in their bouquets, as the ultimate symbol of fidelity. In more recent times, however, the wallflower has become synonymous with a lady sitting out a dance for lack of partners, so would be less popular in wedding decorations.

Another unusual floral token carried by a bride might be a white hollyhock. A popular cottage garden flower, they were oriental in origin, and the sage Chinese claimed the many-seeded pod was an agent of fecundity.

Grooms invariably tuck a rosebud or carnation in the buttonhole of their wedding jacket today — again, more obscure choices would have been made in the past. For instance, veronica and speedwell were a charm to ensure the fidelity of his new wife. Similarly, a witch might advise him to clasp yarrow in his right hand as the bride said "I do"; being a magic herb, it would ensure she would care for him for seven years, at least.

Myrtle was traditionally used for bridal bouquets and head-dresses, though this custom was changed during the reign of the Stuart kings when orange-blossom came to favour. Notwithstanding that the fruit had long symbolised fertility, one wonders whether the fate of the pretty orange-seller, Nell Gwyn, intensified their popularity. Not content with eating the fruit and wearing the flowers to ensure they bore many children, Italian brides wore the floral essence as a perfume, too. Quite costly to produce, it was first made for the princess of Nerola who used it to perfume the gloves she wore on her wedding day — hence the name 'neroli'.

The sunny yellow marigold's country name was "Summer's Bride" for its habit of faithfully following the sun's progress through the sky. They were particular favourites in nuptial posies and the petals were brewed in mead or wine by English country folk to be served to the new bride and thus strengthen her for the night ahead. On the other side of the world, Hindu women attempting to conceive would wear garlands of marigolds, plaintain and betel leaves at Deepavali, the ceremony of light and life.

The carnation's name is said to derive from the word 'coronation' — medieval couples were 'crowned' with this flower and drank wine known as 'sops-in-wine' in which carnation petals were floated at the wedding feast.

Rosemary has long been an emblem of friendship, love and fidelity, so it is customary to tuck a piece into a bridal headband or bouquet. This tradition commenced during Tudor times — when Anne of Cleves arrived as the bride of Henry VIII, she wore a gold coronet, set full of little gilded branches of rosemary. The carved boxes and chests containing her dowry were also made of rosemary wood. During the reign of Elizabeth I, one of her maids commented on a country wedding they had attended at Kenilworth Castle, where:

> "... each ... had a branch of broom tied to his left arm, for rosemary was scant there."

Bridal couples would exchange rosemary sprigs for long-lasting happiness, and as a charm against the evil eye before and after the ceremony. According to English tradition, friends of the bride would all clasp rosemary in their right hand as she came into the church — by doing so, they averred she was indeed chaste.

Get Me to the Church in Time

> "It has been said that a bride's attitude towards her husband may be summed up in three words — Aisle. Altar. Hymn."
> Frank Muir, Denis Norden

It is now generally considered unlucky for the bride and groom to see each other on the wedding morning before they meet in the church. This, however, was not always the case — in the pre-motor car days, the wedding party would walk to and fro from the church with the attendants, and this constituted part of the ceremony.

When leaving for the church (and later, when setting out on their honeymoon) the bridal couple must take care to leave by the front door. This custom derives from the fact that the front door was only ever opened on ceremonial occasions, with ordinary comings and goings being conducted at a side or back door to the house. It is especially significant to enter the house for the first time via the front door, as this augurs well for the beginning of the couple's life together.

On her way to the church, an English bride is lucky if she sees a chimney sweep. In fact, a sweep was sometimes paid to attend weddings so that the bride could kiss his grimy face for luck. This superstition is a relic of the old idea that ashes and soot are a fertility charm, with ashes from ritual fires being spread over newly-planted soil to ensure a good harvest. In fact, records have it that just before he married the then Princess Elizabeth Prince Philip shook hands with a nearby sweep, to guarantee luck in his future life.

In India, it is considered very lucky for a man to meet a female dwarf and his bride to meet a male dwarf on their way to their wedding, while a toad on the church path is another omen for luck and prosperity in Britain. However, not every animal smiled on the bridal pair. Hares were unlucky — for they are believed to be disguised witches. There are many tales of unfortunate old women, possibly disliked by their neighbours, who were found injured after the wounding of a hare. In Cornwall, legend has it that white hares are actually the souls of girls who have died of broken hearts, having been jilted by their lovers — so a bride should quickly look away if she saw one, for it would bring bad luck to her marriage.

Lizards were unlucky in Europe and so were pigs, for these animals were selected by Satan as disguises when he visited mankind. In China, however, pigs meant very good fortune indeed, and a man would present a pig to his lady as a declaration of his intent. He would hope that she would then make him a gift of a jellied foot, which would mean that she accepted his suit. Should things progress well, they could expect to eat pickled pork and drink rice wine out of the cups tied together to symbolise their union at their marriage. Traditionally, Chinese would also sacrifice a pig for the 'dragon' to eat on their wedding day, thus appeasing any anger from the 'dragon god' or emperor.

Miscellaneous superstitions warn the bridal party to avoid policemen, doctors, lawyers, funeral corteges or blind men on their way to church. Once there, they must be careful not to pass through the lych gate, which is closely associated with funerals. Older churches in England often have two gates for this reason — one called the Corpse Gate, the other the Bride Gate.

In approaching the altar, fate could still deal a nasty blow. It is an ill omen if a clock chimes during the ceremony; similarly, a malicious member of the wedding party at an African wedding party should be watched lest they open and close a pair of scissors while the groom is making his vows, for this will render the couple childless.

It is unlucky if the groom drops the ring during the service and he should not endeavour to pick it up. It is only safe if the person who is conducting the ceremony retrieves it, otherwise the life of the couple is ill-omened.

If the church bell makes a strange, hollow sound sometimes when no one has touched it, this indicates the early death of the bride or the groom. However, if the service is safely completed, the ordinary peal of the bell foretells good fortune, for it frightens away the evil spirits which gather at important moment's in a man's life.

At a Turkish wedding, the couple would ask each other riddles after the ceremony to test their intelligence and commonsense as a rehearsal for the real problems in married life which they would have to face together. For instance:

> "My first is in apple and also in pear
> My second's in desperate and also in dare
> My third is in sparrow and also in lark
> My fourth is in cashier and also in clerk
> My fifth is in seven and also in ten
> My whole is a blessing indeed unto men."
> Answer: peace

A pagan ritual which has influenced wedding ceremonies in

both East and West has been tree worship. In England, marriages used to be consecrated under sacred oaks and although the Christian church frowned on this practice, newly wed couples wishing to have the blessings of both worlds would hurry from the altar to dance three times around such a tree, if nearby; often, they would carve a cross or fish into the trunk, thus marking it for other couples in the future. Even today, a photographer will usually usher the bride and groom from the church porch to a nearby tree for that first official photo.

If they are travelling to their new home for the reception, they should choose grey mares to pull the carriage, though of course it does not augur well if they refuse to proceed or stop suddenly. Ditto the colour choice for a car — grey, silver or white are the luckiest choices.

As they make their way to their next destination, the couple may also have old shoes thrown after them, or tied to their wedding vehicle. The use of shoes as a sign of authority, fertility and good luck dates from early Anglo-Saxon times, when the father transferred his authority over his daughter by giving his new son-in-law one of her shoes. The boy would then lightly touch his bride on the head with it, to show he was her new master. He might even, to really make his point, place the shoe firmly at the foot of the honeymoon bed.

In olden days, parents would pay an eligible bachelor to take an unmarried daughter off their hands in exchange for a large dowry. This was not always necessary, and enthusiastic young men did not always wait to be asked, sweeping the girl from her parents' home by force. His partner in crime is represented at modern weddings by the 'best man'. Bridesmaids are also relics from such times — their presence was originally to deter marauders who might try to carry off the bride. Happy is the bride with a matron of honour in her party, for she graces her friend's marriage with particularly happy luck.

As the newly married pair safely leave the church — taking care to leave by the same door they entered — they are usually pelted with rice or confetti for luck. This custom is the remnant of ancient fertility rites when corn and wheat were used to ensure both the prosperity and fruitfulness of the marriage. Nuts, as symbols of new life, were also important — in ancient Rome, walnuts were given to the bride and groom on their wedding day; in France, they were showered with nuts while still kneeling at the altar and the floor of the room where the wedding breakfast was held was strewn with them. Tradition has it that in Devonshire, a bride is greeted as she leaves the church by an old woman who has had many children, who gives her a bag of hazelnuts, as she says "Plenty nuts, plenty cratches" (cradles).

Another old English custom which has not entirely died out is for the bride and groom to negotiate some obstacle as they leave the church — for instance, guests would hold sticks in their way, or ropes of flowers that they had to jump over. In Ireland, a very old stone known as the 'petting stone' was used. The bride would hop over the stone, signifying that she was leaving all her bad moods or 'pets' behind her and leaping into a new life. A variation on the ceremony is found in Birmingham, where the groom has to lift his bride over the locked church gate. He then pays the vicar a toll, to open the gate and let the rest of the party through, which is spent on ale to toast the couple's health.

Shoes, as a symbol of the womb, are a fortunate omen for newly-weds. In Italy, a single white satin slipper is thrown at the couple as they leave the church and it is considered a very fine omen if it actually hits the bride, being a charm that she will have many children — probably a folk memory of ancient bride capture and the attendant struggle. It is also interesting that, although it is now the custom for modern brides to throw their bouquet to unmarried guests in the belief that the one who catches it will be the first to marry, originally she would have thrown her right shoe.

The Wedding Feast

In some parts of the world, there are still people who believe the act of eating together is so sacred that a man and woman will only ever share a meal on their wedding day. Pacific Islanders, for instance, say that sharing the wedding cake constitutes the entire ceremony. However, for many brides, negotiating hazards as they leave the church is only a 'warm up' for the rituals surrounding a traditional wedding feast.

The wedding cake has been the most important feature of the nuptial celebrations, symbolising fertility, good luck and a happy future for the married couple, as evidenced by this rhyme from the Elizabethan era:

> "Today, my Julia, thee must make
> for mistress bride an wedding cake
> Kneade but the dow and it will be
> turned into prosperitie by thee;
> And now the paste of almonds fine,
> Assures a broode o'childer nine."

The wedding cake originated from the ancient Roman 'conferreatio', which comprised salt, water and flour; it was eaten as part of the wedding ceremony while both the bride and groom held three ears of wheat, symbolising plenty. On the other wide of the world, the American Iroquois Indian tribe prepared a wedding cake of wheaten flour too, making the mixture as rich as possible to signify abundance. The tribe's witch doctor would inspect the cake for demons and anoint it with a lucky salve before the bride offered it to her husband.

The Greeks initiated the custom of dropping a coin or ring into the wedding cake mixture just before baking — whoever found it was able to claim a forfeit of his choice from the groom. They also served little sesame cakes at wedding feasts as a fructifying influence, harking back many hundreds of years to when the poet Menander referred to sesame as 'the most fruitful of all seeds'. Sesame and almonds later featured in the recipe for biscuits served to wedding guests in the Middle Ages, which contained eggs, milk, currants, spices and syrup — being the forerunner to the traditional fruit mince we know today.

In ancient Macedonia, the bride-to-be kneaded the dough for her elaborate cake herself, while her little brother stood by with the family's ceremonial sword to frighten away demons that might try to hide in the cake. In nearly every other culture, however, the wedding cake has to be made by a female in the family other than the bride. It is usually said to be very bad luck if the bride takes any part in the making of the cake and she should not even taste it before her wedding day, or she will quickly lose her husband's love.

When preparing the cake, it is most important to stir the mixture clockwise. This belief has its roots in ancient sun worship. The sun, the source of all earthly life and fertility, seems to go from east to west, and its worshippers did likewise on every ritual occasion. To stir a wedding cake 'widdershins', or anti-clockwise, would invite witches to bring dire misfortune to the pair. (For the same reason, Scottish bridal parties often walked sunwise around the church for luck, after the formal ceremony.)

The custom of the bride and groom cutting the first slice of the wedding cake together is to show that they intend to share everything between them. Superstition warns that if the bridegroom attempts to do it on his own, then the marriage will be childless. It is unlucky for anyone to refuse a slice of cake — both for the person concerned, and for the newly-weds.

The bride of today is lucky to be able to simply cut her wedding cake. In early times, the cake would have been literally broken over her head, while guests scrambled for the luck-bringing fragments. In Scotland, this practice was even more hazardous, with an actual plate of iced shortbread and cake being broken on the poor lass's skull. Omens were read from the way the plate broke, the number of pieces signifying the number of children she would have. Sympathies must go to the new bride, should she truthfully fend off her husband's advances that evening by claiming a headache.

In Yorkshire, a piece of wedding cake would be thrown from an upper-storey window as the bride left for her honeymoon and an almost universal country custom requires the bride to visit her family's bee-hive to inform the little creatures of her marriage and leave them a plate of cake. If, after she had done so, the bees start to buzz contentedly, then her marriage will be happy. The bride should also take care to keep a portion of the cake uneaten in a safe place, for then her husband will remain faithful to her. At one time, such portions were kept until the birth of the first child, and then eaten at the christening feast.

The sage Chinese started the tradition of distributing slices of wedding cake to guests and absent friends, so that all might share in the couple's happiness and wish them well for the future. Unmarried men and women receiving a piece can follow the old custom of sleeping with it under their pillows to bring dreams of a future marriage partner. A more elaborate ritual was to break off a fragment of cake, pass it three times through a wedding ring while whispering the wedding service from the Bible, and then sleep on it.

Not all wedding cakes are necessarily of the fruit-brandy-and-marzipan variety, however. At ancient Anglo-Saxon weddings, big baskets of tiny, bite-sized cakes made from honey syrup and clover pollen were distributed to each guest. They were not to be eaten until at least a month had passed after the wedding, by which time they would have fermented richly. In China, the groom gives away quantities of spiced egg buns which have been tinted red — again, they must not be eaten immediately. Amongst Hindus and Melanesians, the doughy cake is only a protective covering for quantities of aromatic and slightly narcotic betel nuts. Chewing these nuts has been enjoyed since Chinese emperors first recorded their use in elaborate manuscripts in 1000 B.C. Since then, they have been used in black magic as a powerful talisman, in marriage and religious ceremonies as a token of affection and peace and as a gesture of hospitality and friendship to wedding guests.

Most recently, the charming French croque-en-bouche has become very popular. Tradition says that this cake developed as a result of the following custom: each wedding guest would bring a small round bun to the wedding, piling them up in a mound in the room where the festivities were to be held. The bride and groom would then be dared to lean over the pile and kiss, without disturbing the mound. If they were successful, they would enjoy a long and happy marriage.

Guests would also take care that the chimney in the festive room had been well swept. Whilst it is lucky to see and touch a sweep en route to the church, it is very unlucky for soot to tumble down the chimney while the wedding feast is in progress.

The French employ another culinary tradition at wedding feasts — they serve chervil (Sweet Cicely) and tarragon soup to the bride and groom. Herbalists often praise chervil for its tonic, strengthening properties and it has long been used as a blood purifier. Wormwood (named Artemisia absinthum, in honour of Artemis, Greek goddess of chastity), was similarly employed to restore vigour, particularly in a timorous bride, and, until quite recently, English country folk would give a bride a posset of marigold petals steeped in honey wine to prepare her for the night ahead. So, thus 'spring-cleaned' and fortified, the happy couple would set out on their life together.

*   *   *

After such a lot of hoop-la, and a day fraught with ceremony and superstition, many a bride may wistfully dream of trading places with a gypsy girl — for their betrothals and marriages were far simpler.

The blackthorn was the bush for young Romany lovers. If a man kisses a girl by this bush, it is as good as a proposal of marriage, particularly if she remembers to take a small sprig and tie it to her caravan or horse's bridle, for it denotes they will have a happy life together.

For the wedding, a broom branch was laid on open ground, and the bride and groom had only to hold hands as they jumped backwards and forwards over it. She would then wear a ring made from river rushes, to be replaced with a gold band bought with the couples' future joint earnings. Even quite recently, nineteenth century navvies and their girls considered themselves legally wed if they jumped to and fro across a birch broom laid across the threshold of their new home.

Simplest of all was the old Anglo-Saxon 'hand-fast' wedding, where the two people concerned held hands and vowed to be faithful for a year. If they no longer cared for each other at the end of this period, they could go their separate ways with little fuss. However, should they wish to make matters permanent, a formal church ceremony could be readily arranged.

BIBLIOGRAPHY

Aikmann, L., *Nature's Healing Arts — from Folk Medicine to Modern Drugs*, National Geographic Books, 1977

Arrowsmith, N. and Moorse, G., *A Field Guide to the Little People*, Macmillan, 1977

Baker, M., *The Gardener's Folklore*, Reader's Union, 1977

Bauer, W.W., *Potions, Remedies and Old Wives' Tales*, Doubleday, 1969

Briggs, K.M., *The Fairies in Tradition and Literature*, Routledge and Kegan Paul, 1967

Brown, R.L., *A Book of Superstitions*, David and Charles Publishers, 1970

Camp, J., *Magic, Myth and Medicine*, Priory Press Ltd., 1973

Chwast, S. and Chewning, E.B., *The Illustrated Flower*, Australia and New Zealand Book Company, 1977

Cohen, J.M. and M.J.,*The Penguin Dictionary of Modern Quotations*, 1985

Comber, L., *Chinese Magic and Superstitions in Malaya*, Eastern Universities Press, 1960

Cribb, A.B. and J.W., *Wild Medicine in Australia*, William Collins, 1981

Doole, L.E., *Herb Magic and Garden Craft*, Sterling, 1972

Francke, E., *The Make-Your-Own Cosmetic and Fragrance Book*, A.H. and A.W. Reed, 1980

Frazier, G. & B., *Aphrodisiac Cookery*, Troubadour Press, 1970

Garland, S., *The Herb and Spice Book*, Frances Lincoln, 1979

Green, J., *A Dictionary of Contemporary Quotations* Pan Books, 1982

Hagger, J., *Australian Colonial Medicine*, Rigby Press, 1979

Hall, D., *The Book of Herbs*, Angus & Robertson, 1972

Harrop, R. (ed.), *Encyclopaedia of Herbs*, Marshall Cavendish, 1977

Harrowven, J., *Origins of Rhymes, Songs and Sayings*, Kaye and Ward, 1977

Hermann, M., *Herbs and Medicinal Flowers*, Galahad Books, 1973

Kamm, M.W., *Old Time Herbs for Northern Gardens*, Dover Publications, 1971

Leavesley, J.H., *Mystique, Magic and Medicine*, ABC Books, 1987

Lehner, E. and J., *Folklore and Odysseys of Food and Medicinal Plants*, Farrar, Straus and Giroux, 1973

Leung, A.Y., *Chinese Herbal Remedies*, Wildwood House, 1985

Leyel, Mrs. C.F., *Elixirs of Life*, Stuart and Watkins Ltd., 1970

Mayhew, A., *The Rose — Myth, Folklore and Legend*, New English Library, 1979

The Concise Oxford Dictionary of Quotations Oxford University Press, 1981

Philpotts, B., *The Book of Fairies*, Ballantine, 1978

Pickston, M., *The Language of Flowers*, Beric Press, U.K. 1968

Powell, C., *The Meaning of Flowers*, Jupiter Books, 1977

Radford, E. and M.A. and Hole, C. (eds), *Encyclopaedia of Superstitions*, Hutchinson and Co., 1961

Folklore, Myths and Legends of Great Britain, Readers' Digest Association, 1979

Reid, S., *Herbs for Australian Gardens and Kitchens*, Rigby Ltd., 1978

Sawyers, M. and Reusswig, W., *The Book of the Far East*, Odhams, 1966

Smith, K.V., *The Illustrated Earth Garden Herbal*, Nelson, 1978

Turner, N., *Aphrodisiacs, Food for Love*, Latimer: New Dimensions, 1975

Thompson, W.A., *Herbs that Heal*, Adam and Charles Black, 1976

Waring, P., *A Dictionary of Omens and Superstitions*, Souvenir Press, 1978

Wheelwright, E.G., *Medicinal Plants and their History*, Dover Publications, 1974